Gayle Graham Yates

**Lotus
Among the
Magnolias**

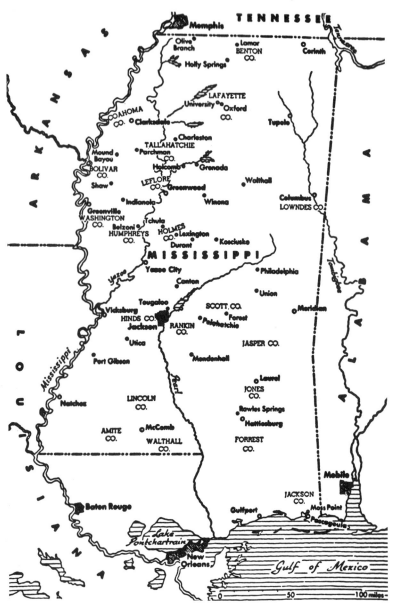

MAP OF MISSISSIPPI The Mississippi Delta, a rich alluvial plain formed by the flood deposits of the Mississippi and Yazoo Rivers, is located in the northwest corner of the state.

Lotus Among the Magnolias

THE MISSISSIPPI CHINESE

by Robert Seto Quan

In Collaboration with
Julian B. Roebuck

Foreword by Stanford M. Lyman

UNIVERSITY PRESS OF MISSISSIPPI

JACKSON

*This volume
has been sponsored by
Mississippi State University.*

Library of Congress Cataloging in Publication Data

Quan, Robert Seto.
  Lotus among the magnolias.

  Bibliography: p.
  Includes index.
  1. Chinese Americans—Mississippi—History.
2. Mississippi—Race relations. I. Roebuck,
Julian B. II. Title.
F350.C5036   976.2'004951   81-23991
ISBN 0-87805-156-2   AACR2

In memory of my father,
Louis Pang Seto,
a pioneer to the Gold Mountain
and now a cosmic ancestral guide

Foreword

The Chinese of the Mississippi Delta comprise one of the far-flung outposts of the Chinese diaspora. Scattered over most of the world in the last four centuries, a portion of the Chinese people is separated—probably forever—from the mainland of China. Chinese communities are to be found from Annam to Zanzibar and in almost all lands and islands in between. Their settlements are cultural islands as well; for the immigrant Chinese and their descendants are remarkable for their collective independence, preservation of homeland customs, and maintenance of traditional social organization in a variety of alien environments. Accused of refusing to assimilate, the overseas Chinese in fact give vivid testimony to the resilience and adaptability of their old world institutions. In America as elsewhere, the Chinese attest to the validity of pluralism.

The Chinese of the Mississippi Delta, however, are unique; their community stands out from those established by their ethnic compatriots in San Francisco, New York City, Los Angeles, Chicago or Vancouver, British Columbia. In the large cities of North America, Chinese established an "extra-territorial" enclave within the urban setting. Called "Chinatowns," these communities are not only products of racism and segregation; they also represent the congregative spirit of the Cantonese immigrants and the transplantation of "premodern," local institutions to "modern" cosmopolitan America. Chinatown is not merely a ghetto with pagodas and a paper dragon; it is a complex of traditional institutions,—a culture, an economy, and a way of life—that is separate and thriving in America. The Chinatown Chinese are known to white American tourists— and to Blacks, Japanese, Pilipinos, and Hispanics—as persevering ethnics who provide food, curios, and an exotic scene for those in search of the unusual. But to the *Delta Lotus* Chinese —the Chinese of Mississippi surveilled in the present study— the Chinatown Chinese are also strange. Huddled together in crowded streets, noisy bars and restaurants, and cramped quarters, the Chinatown *Hon Yen* do not impress the second and third generation Chinese Americans from Leflore, Quitman, Sharkey, Sunflower and the six other counties of the Mississippi Delta. Chinese from the Deep South do not speak the same English, dress in the same style, walk in the same manner, or think in the same way as Chinatowners. Nor are they indistinguishable from America's middle class urbanites. The *Delta Lotus* is a new variety of flora in the American ethnic garden. It currently flourishes among the magnolias of Mississippi, but only time will tell whether it will wither in the rice bowl of urban Chinatowns or flower among the other species in Northern cities and suburbs.

One central fact makes the Mississippi Chinese exceptional to their counterparts in urban America. There is no Chinatown in the Mississippi Delta. These Chinese have been cut off from the religious, medical, educational, familial, village, and communal institutions that Cantonese brought with them to America. Most significant there are no clans, *hui kuan* (speech and locality associations), secret societies and temples established among the Delta Chinese. Such institutions are the mainstay of the overseas Chinatown—not only in the United States, but throughout Southeast Asia, Oceania, and Africa. The Mississippi Chinese have forged a community without these traditional forms of organization. They have constructed their community around two other institutions: the nuclear family and the family-centered grocery store.

The Delta Chinese have been able to create their own type of community, first, because of the presence of sufficient women among them to make marriage and domesticity possible; second, because they took up a strategic if unwanted position between the white and black populations, providing goods and services to the latter, while preserving and protecting the caste superiority of the former.

The shortage of women has been the bane of most overseas Chinese communities. In the United States the number of Chinese males was almost twenty times greater than females in 1890. In the Chinatowns of San Francisco, New York, Chicago and other large cities homeless men clubbed together in sur-name associations, *Landsmannschaften,* and clandestine criminal-political societies, and recreated themselves in broth-els and gambling parlors, and, on occasion, with opium. Money was sent to patiently waiting wives in China. Sons sired on occasional visits to the homeland were encouraged to follow their fathers to the overseas Chinatown, creating generations of familial separation. As a largely male community, the China-towns of America—from 1850 until 1940—survived despite their family-less condition. Secret societies owned or controlled brothels where declassé Chinese women were pressed into in-dentured service as prostitutes. America's harsh anti-Chinese immigration laws—which from 1882 until 1943 prohibited *in-ter alia* the entrance of a Chinese laborer's wife—were partially circumvented by the smuggling of Chinese into America. But the imbalance in the sex ratio was not ended until 1970.

The Mississippi Chinese—who settled in that area from the middle 1870s—appear to have suffered from the shortage of women during the first fifty years of their habitation there. Aspects of their marital problems are indicated in the common-law marriages of a few Delta Chinese to black women and in the abortive attempt by the *Ong Leng Tong*—a secret society —to organize among them. However, enough women seem to have arrived to make the establishment of Chinese families possible after 1920. One wonders whether these women were illegal entrants or, more likely, the wives of Chinese merchants —one of the classes whose spouses were exempt from the re-strictions of the Chinese Exclusion Act. These women—as the testimony of the Chinese in the present study reveals in count-less ways—functioned to create a stable family-centered com-munity. They became wives and mothers to the Delta Chinese, and by making hearth and home possible obviated the necessity of clans, *hui kuan,* and secret societies, and of whoring, gam-bling, and drug-taking. Moreover, these women undertook and largely succeeded in resolving the most significant problem facing their people in the South—making the Chinese respect-able in the eyes of local Mississippians. Their major project in this regard was the establishment of the Chinese Baptist Church. A *Christian* identity established the trustworthiness and probity of the Chinese merchant; for, as Max Weber had observed in his travels through the American South in 1904, baptism was the single most important prerequisite to economic and social acceptance in backwoods America's version of the Protestant ethic. A *Chinese* Christian identity—implemented by means of a separate church—helped to lift the hated epithet "colored" from the Chinese and elevated them above the Negroes.

The children born of these intra-racial marriages also helped to solidify the Chinese group and deter its amalgamation with the Blacks. Ironically the very fact that these children were citizens of the United States by reason of their birth in America —while their immigrant parents remained "aliens ineligible to citizenship" until 1943—caused them to suffer the rigors of segregated schooling. When Mrs. Gong Lum brought suit in the United States Supreme Court in 1927 to prevent her children from being sent to the school for "colored" children, she was told by the Court that she could not avail herself of the equal treatment clauses of the Burlingame Treaty between the United States and China because they applied only to Chinese aliens. After that ignominious setback, many Delta Chinese sent their children to the private Baptist school, further entrenching their acceptable religious identification and keeping them apart from Negro children.

The Chinese community in the Delta is not territorially compact. Much of it consists of grocery stores, with residences in the rear, scattered throughout the Black sections of the several counties. The Chinese grocer developed much of the character that Werner Sombart attributed to the economic stranger. Rational calculation and a perceptive scrutiny of the socio-cultural realities of the Southern racial situation provided the basis for his everyday conduct. These included paying scrupulous attention to the prevailing etiquette of race relations that supported the caste structure, teaching, but not believing in, the praxiological precepts of Mississippi racialism to their children, and purchasing personal security and the right to a livelihood with carefully calculated donations to all factions embroiled in racial struggles. Despite its location within the black community or in the racially undefined border areas between whites and blacks, the Chinese community has not been absorbed by either racial group. Rather, it has emerged out of an attempt to conflate it with the low-caste group into a racial quasi-caste in its own right. The key to this emergence has been *respectability*—a status attained by religious conversion and carefully maintained public neutrality in the civil rights struggle.

The Delta Chinese identify themselves in a complex status structure based on deference, reference, and place. Deference is accorded on the basis of age and pioneer experience in settling in the Delta. Reference is based on Delta Chinese identity as either aged first families, aging local businessmen, adult middle class professionals who might leave the area but not escape their Mississippi roots, and young people whose future seems bound up with that of their nearest age group, the professionals. Place is always the Delta, for these Chinese are neither one more group of Chinese Americans nor a people dissolved in the melting pot. When the professionals and youth leave Mississippi for the big cities of the North, West, or New South, they discover how much they are emotionally, linguistically, and culturally tied to the region of their birth. These Chinese are the lotus that has its roots in the bottomland of the Mississippi Delta.

Yet, as the testimony of the young Chinese American women of the Delta reveals, the Chinese community of Mississippi is again threatened by the loss of its distaff group. These women are better educated than their parents or grandparents, and, unlike their less adventurous male peers, willing to strike out on their own—in the big cities, in the new careers opening up for women, and, most significantly, in intermarriages with white men of their own class and aspiration. The young Mississippi Chinese revere their aged women pioneers and preservers of culture. But they do not wish to emulate them. For the females of the Delta Lotus it seems time to pull up roots, transplant the seedlings, and generate new and different varieties.

The Chinese of the Mississippi Delta are part of the rich and variegated history and culture of the Deep South. Their part in the caste and class structure of this region has not been given its due—except by the Mississippi Chinese themselves and by the blacks and whites who, sometimes grudgingly, sometimes gratefully, acknowledge their presence. This is their story. Their words, so carefully and lovingly collected by Robert Seto Quan and edited and interpreted with the aid of Julian B. Roebuck, tell a saga of Chinese diaspora in America.

Stanford M. Lyman
Professor of Sociology and Asian Studies
New School for Social Research

Preface

In writing about the Chinese community of the Mississippi Delta, we have been conscious of two differences between the present investigation and other studies of Chinese Americans. First, most studies have focused on large urban settlements supported by cultural centers ("Chinatowns") and by continuous immigration. In contrast, we portray a small, isolated enclave situated within a biracial society—a small Southern town —and lacking the benefit of ethnic cultural centers or of significant immigration. Second, other reports on Delta Chinese Americans have been written by people unable to claim any affiliation with the society they studied, whose point of view was therefore necessarily limited. The information for the present book was collected firsthand by Robert Quan, who speaks both Cantonese and English. As a Chinese American he was afforded access to the community that would not have been granted to someone of another ethnic background.

Quan lived in the Chinese Delta community from 1975 through 1978 while he taught at Delta State University in Cleveland, Mississippi. He shared in the lives of the Chinese people during this period, recording his personal observations of their social life and daily work. His field notes recorded the interviews and conversations quoted throughout this book and are supplemented by the photographs he took at the time. No tape recordings were made, and pseudonyms have been used to protect the privacy of individuals within the Chinese community. The data gathered have been organized and interpreted by both authors, but the first-person narrative, used in chapters 2–7, refers to fieldwork performed by the senior author alone.

From preliminary observations and information given to him by friends who were leaders in the Delta Chinese community, Quan found that the Delta Chinese divided themselves into five major categories: *Lo Nen Ga* (old people), *Sen Ga* (businessmen), *Jen Ga* (professionals), *Hok San* (college students), and *Ching Nen* (young people). The Chinese describe their community and themselves by reference to these naturally occurring groups. We have therefore used them to organize our account, much as the Chinese use them to define their collective and individual identity. One chapter has been devoted to each reference group, and about each we have asked the following questions: Who are the members? How did they become members? How do they view themselves and other groups? How do they define and perceive the world around them? How do they envision life and survival inside and beyond the Mississippi Delta? What are their hopes and concerns?

The first Chinese immigrants to the Delta were classified as "colored."[1] They and members of the second and third generations managed to transform this pejorative identity tag and to establish a functional Chinese community. Their search for identity as Mississippi Chinese and as Americans occurred against a background of shifting economic pressures and changing race relations. It is the story of this search that we have tried to tell, with the help of many of the individuals who have lived it. We hope that our attempt to trace the vicissitudes of life among three Mississippi Delta Chinese generations will prove interesting and useful to laymen, students of ethnic group relations, and the Mississippi Chinese themselves. Though our findings suggest that these remarkable people will eventually disperse, we also note some of the contributions that their culture will leave behind. American civilization is richer as a result of their presence as a community.

The senior author thanks the American Sociological Association and Minority Fellowship Program directors, Phil Carey and Paul Williams, for a $5,000 Sydney S. Spivack Fellowship award, which facilitated the research on which this book is based. John H. Peterson, James B. Cowie, and Stanford M. Ly-

---

[1]Not to be confused with the term "colored" used to designate blacks; "colored Chinese" is a separate classification.

man contributed their sage counsel during fieldwork. Both authors are grateful to several members of the Chinese community, including Gwen Gong, who read, edited, and criticized the findings. We also thank the many white, black, and Chinese Mississippians who gave us essential information.

The senior author extends his gratitude to Lou Git, Jennifer Mei Lin, Dave, Kathy, Shell, Stan, and Dexter of the Quan family; and to Fay Tuey and Dr. Barry Eckhouse for their patience and encouragement from start to finish. Sue Yong Seto provided motherly wisdom and pecuniary aid, and Elizabeth Roebuck provided excellent nutritional support. Both authors wish to thank Barney McKee and Seetha Srinivasan of the University Press of Mississippi and Lyell Behr of Mississippi State University for their support. We dedicate this book to Robert Quan's late father, Louis Pang Seto.

Robert Seto Quan   *Los Angeles, California*
Julian B. Roebuck   *Mississippi State University*

Lotus
Among the
Magnolias

CHAPTER ONE

Introduction

The Mississippi Delta, a rich alluvial plain formed by the flood deposits of the Mississippi and Yazoo rivers, is located in the northwest corner of the state. It is usually considered to stretch over a 185-mile distance from the lobby of the Peabody Hotel in Memphis, Tennessee, to Catfish Row in Vicksburg, Mississippi (though neither of these two cities is included in a strict geographical description of the Delta). The area extends sixty miles east of the Mississippi River and includes approximately a sixth of the state's land and a fifth of its population.

The white planter still sits at the apex of the Delta's social hierarchy, with the blacks at the bottom. Despite the present-day decrease in agricultural labor requirements, blacks are more concentrated in this region than in any other part of the state. The stereotype of the inhabitants frequently focuses on the polarization of these two groups. The Chinese, a small community whose social niche falls between the whites and blacks of all social classes are often overlooked. Unlike most Chinese immigrants elsewhere, they are isolated and have no access to Chinese schools, Buddhist temples, Chinese clan and lineage organizations, Chinese literature and media, Chinese stores, apothecaries, theaters, museums, or markets. Moreover, the young adult Chinese of the region frequently migrate to other areas, while few Chinese Americans move in to replace them.

According to the U.S. Census there were 1,244 Chinese Americans in Mississippi in 1960 and 1,441 in 1970. The 1980 preliminary census reports indicate that 1,835 Asians and Pacific Islanders live in the state.[1] At present there is no way to

[1] U.S. Bureau of the Census, *U.S. Census of Population: 1960*, vol. 1, "Characteristics of Population, Part 26, Mississippi" (Washington, D.C.: U.S. Government Printing Office, 1967), pp. 26–82-26-87. Of the 1,244 Chinese in

determine the number of Chinese in this category. Still, it may be said that the Chinese represent a very small population within Mississippi and that most live in the Delta towns of Greenville, Cleveland, Clarksdale, and Greenwood. Most other Southern Chinese Americans live in counties adjacent to the Delta in the states of Tennessee, Arkansas, and Louisiana. We may well ask how they came to the Delta. We know little historically about the Chinese in Mississippi prior to 1910.[2] Loewen found archival data about Chinese coolies who were imported from China during the Reconstruction period in Mississippi (1866–1876). During this time in the state's history, blacks were voting Republican and were seeking to improve their socioeconomic position following Emancipation. Their movement from

---

Mississippi in 1960, 1,115 lived in the Delta. There are ten counties included in the Delta Mississippi area: Bolivar, Coahoma, Humphreys, Issaquena, Leflore, Quitman, Sharkey, Sunflower, Tunica, and Washington. The Delta also cuts into parts of the following counties: Desoto, Holmes, Panola, Tate, Tallahatchie, Warren, and Yazoo. The total (1,115) reflects population in all seventeen counties. U.S. Bureau of the Census, *Census of Population: 1970, Subject Reports,* PC (2)–1G, "Japanese, Chinese, and Fillipinos in the United States," Supplementary Report, "Race of the Population of the United States, by States: 1970," PC (S1)–11 (Washington, D.C.: U.S. Government Printing Office, 1972), p. 1–293. Of the 1,441 Chinese in Mississippi in 1970, 1,108 lived in the Delta. See U.S. Bureau of the Census, *U.S. Census of Population: 1970,* vol. 1, "Characteristics of Population, Part 26, Mississippi" (Washington, D.C.: U.S. Government Printing Office 1973) pp. 26–84–26–86. U.S. Bureau of the Census, *Census of Population,* Supplementary Report, PC 80–S1–3 (Washington, D.C.: U.S. Government Printing Office, 1981), p. 7. Of the 1,835 Chinese in Mississippi, in 1981, 1,718 Asian/Pacific Islanders lived in the Delta. See U.S. Bureau of the Census, *1980 Census of Population and Housing,* "Advance Reports: Mississippi, Final Population and Housing Count," PHC 80–V–26 (Washington, D.C.: U.S. Government Printing Office, 1981), pp. 4–15.

[2] There have been only four studies of the Mississippi Chinese by sociologists: Robert W. O'Brien, "Status of the Chinese in the Mississippi Delta," *Social Forces* (March 1941), pp. 386–390; George A. Rummel III, "The Delta Chinese: An Exploratory Study in Assimilation" (master's thesis, University of Mississippi, Oxford, 1966); Kit-Mui Leung Chan, "Assimilation of the Chinese Americans in the Mississippi Delta" (master's thesis, Mississippi State University, Starkville, 1969); James W. Loewen, *The Mississippi Chinese: Between Black and White* (Cambridge, Mass.: Harvard University Press, 1971). These works, although illuminating, stress an outsider's view of the Mississippi Chinese and their adjustment to the American scene. Further information bearing on past studies of the Mississippi Chinese and a definitive methodological analysis of the research strategy used in this study can be found in Robert Seto Quan, "A Temporal Ethnography of the Mississippi Chinese: The Maintenance/Dissolution of an Ethnic Enclave" (Ph.D. dissertation, Mississippi State University, Starkville, 1978).

one plantation to another in search of better working arrangements infuriated some planters. As a result Southern Delta cotton planters encouraged European and Yankee white immigrants to come to the Delta as sharecroppers. When such efforts failed, they initiated a campaign to bring Chinese immigrants to the cotton lands of Mississippi, Arkansas, and Louisiana. Planters organized conventions and solicited the help of newspapers such as the *Vicksburg Times* in support of a movement for the importation of oriental labor.[3] It was hoped that coolies (who without citizenship could be expected to be apolitical) would either displace black labor or would force blacks to resume their former submission.

The scheme to import Chinese coolies was debated vigorously in *De Bow's Review*. The journal's editor, William M. Burwell, opposed coolie importation, basing his views on his estimate that the attempt to use coolie labor to compete with England in the production of agricultural raw materials was economically futile.

The forces favoring coolie importation won, and in July 1869 a labor convention met in Memphis, Tennessee, to consider importing Chinese to work in the cotton, sugar, rice, and tobacco fields. *De Bow's Review* (1869–1870) reported that Cornelius Koopmanschap, a Dutch sea captain who was present at the convention, had declared that his steamers could transport Chinese to California and had done so in the past. With the opening of the Pacific Railroad, coolies would be able to reach the Mississippi Valley in about fifty days at a per person cost of about one hundred dollars. The St. Louis and Pacific railroads agreed to support Koopmanschap's plan.

Thus encouraged, Koopmanschap, accompanied by a Chinese recruiter, Tye Kim Orr, traveled into the interior of Kwangtung Province to secure Chinese who would participate

[3] Powerful interests in the United States supported the plan for importing Chinese labor into the South including the *New York Tribune*, the *New York Journal of Commerce*, the *Southern Farmer*, and the *New Orleans Commercial Bulletin*. See William M. Burwell, "Science and the Mechanic Arts Against Coolies," *De Bow's Review* (July 1869), pp. 557–571; and the discussion in Stanford M. Lyman, "The Structure of Chinese Society in Nineteenth-Century America" (Ph.D. dissertation, Univeristy of California, Berkeley, 1961), pp. 399–404.

5

in the scheme. The two men reasoned that they could find more ignorant and cooperative Chinese coolies there than in coastal Canton. On February 7, 1870, the first cargo of two hundred coolies bound for New Orleans cleared from Hong Kong in the ship *Ville de St. Lo* under charter to Koopmanschap and Company of San Francisco. When the coolies reached New Orleans and learned the true purpose of their enlistment, they jumped ship, scattering in all directions. The "Koopmanschap Experiment" failed. Undoubtedly, the coolie trade to the South would have continued if the British government had not closed the port of Hong Kong in 1870 to all emigrant ships except those trading within the British Empire.[4]

Loewen's research of archival records verifies that during the late 1860s and early 1870s plantation owners eager to displace Negro farm workers did receive some Chinese laborers, whom they employed to pick cotton. Loewen's analysis of the 1880 census showed that fifty-one Chinese were living in Mississippi at this time. These coolies had been recruited from Hong Kong and worked as farm laborers in Washington County. The experiment failed, however. Chinese labor proved to be more expensive and less dependable than black labor; importation was risky and costly; and the imported Chinese quickly lost interest because of exploitation by the planters and low economic returns from the sharecropping land tenure system. The Chinese sojourners wished to make money quickly and to return to China to be with their families. Sharecropping offered no instant rewards.[5]

Some Chinese laborers left the cotton fields early and sought work in Arkansas, Louisiana, and Georgia. Some of those who remained became peddlers and storekeepers. Loewen notes that the decline of the plantation furnish system provided an economic opportunity for the Mississippi Chinese. Planters usually owned a commissary and furnished supplies to their black sharecroppers on credit; this mercantile role enabled planters to make money and to offset losses from natural disasters. Black

[4] Persia Crawford Campbell, *Chinese Coolie Emigration to Countries within the British Empire* (London: King and Sons, 1923); Lyman, "The Structure of Chinese Society."

[5] Loewen, *The Mississippi Chinese.*

6

sharecroppers bought staples (meat, meal, molasses, and clothing) and were enticed to buy luxuries (canned fish, candy, rings, and pins) from commissaries on credit with interest as high as 100 percent. Debts were not settled until after the cotton harvest, at which time the sharecropper sold his cotton back to the plantation at plantation prices. The cost of the sharecropper's goods purchased from the commissary during the work year, plus interest, was subtracted from the sharecropper's portion of the crop. This system operated to keep many blacks in a state of virtual peonage.

Several factors led to a decline of the furnish system. The commissary only offered a limited selection of items, and its credit system destroyed rapport between sharecroppers and planters. Moreover, the requirements for increased agricultural production demanded that swamps be drained and land cleared. Labor engaged to do such work was often paid in cash, and enough money (usually in the form of Mississippi State Script, or "cotton money") was circulating to make a grocery venture feasible. Some Chinese seized the opportunity to make money as small independent merchants and thereby carved their own economic niche in the Delta. Those Chinese who had saved sufficient capital were able to start one-room grocery stores, usually shacks of twenty feet by twenty feet. Wholesale merchants were eager to sell to the Chinese, whom they trusted. Some sojourners prospered and returned to China upon retirement; others fell victim to diseases such as yellow fever and malaria. Still others remained in the Delta.

Quan recorded several accounts given to him by living descendants who trace their family lineage to early Chinese immigrants in the Delta. Wong On was probably the most notable of the earliest Chinese settlers in the Mississippi Delta, but he was not the first Chinese in Mississippi. Still, he was one of the last survivors of the early cohort. According to Wong's daughter, Mrs. Joe Suen Hen (Arlee Sing), Wong was born near Canton, China, in 1844. He came to California in 1860 and worked as a water boy on the Central Pacific segment of the Transcontinental Rail Road (1863–1869). Upon completion of the railroad, he booked passage to Illinois and then worked at another railroad job that brought him through Arkansas to New Orleans.

GROCERY SHACK The decline of the plantation furnish system created an economic opportunity for the Delta Chinese to prosper as independent grocery merchants. By saving money, the Chinese had sufficient capital to start one-room grocery stores, usually 20' X 20' shacks. Living quarters were in the back of the store.

There Wong may have worked in the fisheries or on shrimp farms in New Orleans. At any rate he never worked in the sugar cane fields of Louisiana.

In 1875 Wong and thirteen men came up the Mississippi River to pick cotton in the Delta. They landed in Greenville and met two Chinese who had a store there, Joe Kee and Joe Ly. Not much is known about this group of men, but they probably picked cotton prior to starting grocery stores. Wong and his

8

men perceived little profit from cotton picking, so they moved to Stoneville (near Leland) to a place known as California Plantation. They became tenant farmers or land renters who attempted to sell their cotton independently. Their departure from the sharecropping system met with legal resistance, so they transported their own cotton down to New Orleans for sale. Several other Chinese men joined Wong, and they farmed successfully for three years. In 1878 two men died of yellow fever, and by 1880 several of Wong's men had returned to China.

Wong On took a Negro wife, Emma Clay, in 1881 and opened a store in Stoneville. The couple produced twelve children. Though Wong's immigration name was Charlie Sing, he was called "Captain" by the local residents. He intended to send his daughter, Arlee, back to China to attend school and live with his sister. Unfortunately his sister died before the arrangements were completed. According to Arlee, Wong was a popular man in Stoneville, and Chinese bachelors often came to visit and smoke opium with him. Wong On spent the remainder of his life in Stoneville and in 1943 died peacefully at ninety-nine.

Joe Ting recalls that his great uncle, Joe Gow Nue, came to Mississippi around 1883 following completion of the Southern Pacific Rail Road connecting Los Angeles and New Orleans. Joe Gow Nue may have worked at the Tai Loy Fishery in New Orleans, later supposedly destroyed by fire. In any case, Joe and some Chinese men subsequently took a Mississippi River barge or steamboat for Cairo, Illinois—a port of entry and center for agricultural and industrial products. The boat never reached Cairo but landed instead near Hollandale, Mississippi. Five Chinese men disembarked: Yee went to Arkansas, while three Joes went to Greenwood, Indianola, and Greenville, Mississippi. The fifth man, Wong, was believed to be Wong On and may have been returning from New Orleans on a business trip. What Joe Gow Nue did upon his arrival in the Delta is uncertain. He may have worked in the cotton fields or found an apprenticeship in a Chinese grocery store. We do know that in 1910 Joe Gow Nue bought a grocery store near the Greenville levee from a Chinese man about to return to China. Such a sale was

9

JOE GOW NUE STORE The Joe Gow Nue store circa 1927. It was a 161' X 32' building located at the foot of Washington Street near the Greenville levee. Operating as a service store, customers could phone in orders and have them delivered. The rear of the store housed a kitchen, store room, and five bedrooms for employees.
Courtesy of the Joe Ting Collection

unusual, for in general, Chinese stores were passed down or sold to relatives, many of whom came from outside the Delta.[6]

Many Delta Chinese who are now old people left China for the United States during a period of turmoil following the

[6]Relatives of Joe Ting and James Chow (later Ting's partner) came from Boston to operate the Joe Gow Nue store for about twenty years. It was passed down to Joe Ting by his father about 1937. For further discussion, see Robert Seto Quan, "The Creation, Maintenance, and Dissolution of Mississippi Delta Chinese Identities," *Bulletin, Chinese Historical Society of America,* vol. 16, nos. 3, 4, 5, 6 (March-June 1981).

downfall of the Imperial Manchu dynasty, which was over-thrown by peasant rebellion in 1911. According to Barrington Moore, Jr.,[7] weaknesses in the central government and corruption of the bureaucratic meritocracy after 1900 led to a break-down of the landed gentry. Some members of this class were either coopted by warlords or became warlords themselves. Others exploited the small landowners and turned many of them into uprooted peasant sharecroppers by means of high taxes and interest rates. Rebellions by land-short peasants lasted throughout the Kuomingtang period from 1911 to 1949, when the Communist party took over. By 1920 only 50 percent of the peasants owned any land at all. Most of the dispossessed class became destitute; many starved. Displaced from the village system, many became day laborers, bandits, warlord recruits, and wanderers without money or a sense of place. Some joined the Communist movement after 1921. Still others emigrated.

[7]Barrington Moore, Jr., *The Social Origins of Dictatorship and Democracy: Lord and Peasant in the Making of the Modern World* (Boston: Beacon Press, 1966), pp. 201–227.

The Old People

The Delta Chinese define old people as individuals over sixty years. Of the aged, then, most were born in China and grew up as children on peasant farms in Kwangtung Province. A few claimed to be the children of petty merchants in the city of Canton. Most old people had at one time worked as peasants in China, where they had received only three to five years of grammar school education. Higher education was available only to the wealthy. All of the individuals I met and talked to could read and write Chinese. They had learned English in the United States. All expressed traditional Confucianist views about life in general and the family in particular. They live by a code that demands strong allegiance to the family, deference to elders, respect for the patriarch, endogamous marriages, arranged marriages, and filial piety.[1] They insist on clearly defined sex roles within the family: the man is the provider and the boss, the female a mother and a domestic. Divorce they consider a dishonor to all family members. Not

---

[1] In China the whole Confucian ethic of filial piety was impossible to have without land ownership. Property was scarce among poor peasants, and family life was impossible for the landless: no property, no family, no children. However, in the Delta property ownership and businesses were utilized to maintain filial respect and patrilineality because sons were usually in line to inherit their father's stores, thereby making the transplantation of filial piety viable in the Delta. The third and fourth generations may no longer count on property as a base supporting filial piety. No longer does the aging Chinese proprietor turn the grocery store over to a son (or children) who continues the business—unless, of course, it is a large, thriving store in the white area. The grocer usually sells out and invests his money in the education of his children or in other property. Some few invest in other family businesses, but their children wish to become professionals in most cases rather than businessmen.

surprisingly, no one seeks a divorce. The majority of old Chinese in the Mississippi Delta are women who have outlived their husbands. Widows and widowers unable to run a grocery store any longer live with married children.

The oldest members of the Chinese community came to the Mississippi Delta between 1910 and 1930. Most opened grocery stores or worked for relatives who already owned stores, which today, as in the past, are located chiefly in black neighborhoods and service black customers. A few Chinese own larger and more modern stores in white commercial sections which cater to the general public. Many elderly merchants bought up real property surrounding their stores over the years. Buildings on these properties are frequently rented to white businessmen. Old people explained that these investments were made to take care of the living and educational expenses of families with five or six children. These entrepreneurs are financially well off, that is, they own estates valued at between $60,000 to $175,000 each.

Most old people live in the back of their stores or in adjacent modest homes. Proximity to the workplace is convenient because most do not drive and it permits them to keep an eye on their property. Such living arrangements have also historically precluded conflicts with whites who resist Chinese movement into white neighborhoods (the immigrants have been able to buy real estate in white residential sections only since World War II; therefore the first generation Delta Chinese live either in marginally zoned residential areas or in black neighborhoods). They find it easier and more economically advantageous to add rooms to existing living quarters than to move out or rebuild. Dwelling interiors are nicer in all respects than dwelling exteriors. Grocery stores from the outside look weather-beaten and moderately dilapidated, as do the surrounding commercial buildings. Stores, store living quarters, and houses are not renovated. The Chinese fear that the Caucasians[2]

---

[2] This term was used by some Chinese in referring to whites. Others used the term "white." The term "Caucasian" entered current usage after being used as a legal term in adverse judgments involving the Chinese. See, for example, *Mississippi Reports,* vol. 130, 1925, *Rice et al.* v. *Gong Lum et al.,* p. 763. The U.S. Supreme Court, backing the Mississippi Supreme Court, handed

will resent property improvement and that the blacks will regard it as a sign of wealth. Old commercial milk signs and antiquated porcelain-covered Coca-Cola thermometers attached to the storefronts are left in place because they indicate the store's age-old integrity. Store merchandise is stacked neatly on warped shelves protruding from faded painted walls. Health-care products, medicine boxes, and patent medicines dating to the 1930s and the 1940s decorate unused, dust-covered shelves.

Old people dress conservatively. Women wear plain dark dresses and men wear white short-sleeved shirts and inexpensive dark trousers. Most speak broken English. Nonetheless, they manage to communicate effectively with blacks and whites. All but a few have acquired the linguistic ability to pass the compulsory literacy tests for naturalization.

Old People at Home

Members of this group see themselves at home as a bridge connecting the distant past to the present. As traditional teachers at the top of the community deference hierarchy, they promote the "Chinese way." They realize that their children and grandchildren have to learn American customs in order to be successful, but they dislike the personal cost of the climb, which means to them the casting aside of many Chinese traditions. Old people attempt to perpetuate Chinese culture by passing on knowledge of Chinese art, cuisine, folklore, language, customs, health-care practices, deference titles and salutations, respect for elders, demeanor and etiquette, endogamous marriage, and a patriarchal family system. They also act as caretakers of grandchildren, as business and marital counselors, as marriage go-betweens, as arbitrators of family disputes, and as providers and financial supporters.

The aged accept the status of Chinese immigrants and display a cherished Chinese presence in many different ways. For ex-

down the following decision: "It has been at all times the policy of lawmakers of Mississippi to preserve white schools for members of the Caucasian race alone."

ample, they wear Chinese slippers, jade, and gold jewelry. Many showed me meaningful Chinese objets d'art—oriental rugs, imported copies of art objects of the Ming and Ch'ing (Manchu) dynasties (dating back to A.D. 1415) and Chinese porcelain vases, bowls, and platters (displayed on walls and tables). Scattered about throughout the homes were hand-painted china with gold designs; brass bowls, platters, and urns; ginger jars depicting court and palace scenes; ivory, alabaster, and jade animals carved in high relief (water buffalo, fish, elephants); and figurines of venerable sages indicating good omens. Living rooms were decorated with brush-and-ink drawings of spacious landscapes. Rice paper paintings frequently depicted temples and palaces. Ever present were lifelike watercolor renditions of willows planted along a riverbank and Chinese architecture and landscape paintings on silk. There were intricately embroidered wildlife scenes of white cranes, rabbits, roosters, and tigers. Such furnishings reflect the meaningful cultural past of old people. One elderly woman remarked: "These art pictures remind me of China when I was a child . . ., so peaceful and so full. I hope that my children's children will have this kind of Chinese things in their homes."

This story by an old woman typified old people's concern with Chinese identity:

> I was born here in the United States, but my father decided that I should have Chinese schooling, you know—learn to be a good Chinese girl. I am so sad that I spent all of those four years in Canton city and never saw the beautiful countryside of my China. I will never see it now, but my life here has never been worth it. Perhaps some day my children will see the old country.

Old people view their teachings as meaningful, enduring, and important to their children's survival in the Delta. One old woman specified the necessity of clinging to a Chinese identity for survival purposes.

> I see myself as honored and respected by all of my children and the Chinese community. I know I will not be living much longer. All I hope is that my children and their children's children carry within their hearts the Chinese ways. I have taught my children to be proud of their ancestry, that they are *Hon Yen* [Chinese] and

Chinese ways have lasted for many centuries. I have told them that being Chinese is knowing who they are. This is more precious than all the gold in the world. They must carry this Chinese feeling close to their breast for as long as they live and educate their children as I have done for so many years. Because if they do not, then the Delta and *Lo Fan* [white][3] ways will swallow them up. This knowledge I have given them will help them in the future when I am gone. I know it will. . . .

Another old woman declared her Chinese identity and expressed her hopes that some of the cultural past would linger with her children:

We old people are Chinese and are not really Americans. We came from the old country a long time ago and have raised our children the best way we know how—the Chinese way. My children think of themselves more *Bok Guey* [white] than *Hon Yen* [Chinese]. You know they are *san lai* [primitive] and I understand why . . ., but I think of myself as being Chinese. I know that with each generation much of the Chinese ways will be lost. I cannot help that because my children live in America. But I have spent much time in teaching them the Chinese ways, now not much will be passed on to others. I will die in a few years, but I will live in their memory as a door to the past.

Old people cover their walls with pictures of their children and grandchildren, symbols of their success as parents and grandparents. Photographs of children growing up and getting married and candid snapshots of grandchildren adorn the living room. These pictures and the running commentary on them indicate family pride as well as assimilation to the American way of life. One elderly woman commented:

You see [pointing to a handsome man] that was my husband and these are my children [calling each one by name]. . . . We worked hard in the store and put two of our boys through college. Thank God my husband was still alive then to watch their graduation. You see, like many of the old people, we had our children late in life. Anyway, my two daughters married after graduating and are living in Mississippi. Everyone says that I raised a very good family and those children are very successful now. They have good jobs.

[3]Throughout the pages that follow, several Chinese words are used to denote whites. Each Chinese expression has the following literal translation: *Sai Yen* [westerners], *Bok Guey* [white ghosts or devils], and *Lo Fan* [strangers]. The use of each term by the Chinese suggests the cultural remoteness they feel from the prevailing white society.

I love my children and would do anything for them. My children are my job and happiness in old age.

Old people verbalized a strong conciousness of Chinese racial ancestry and cultural superiority. Frequently they drew a sharp contrast between their Chinese identity and that of the Westerner. During conversations in Chinese with me, with other old people, and with children in Chinese homes, they often commented proudly: "The *Hon Yen* [Chinese], don't forget, are an old civilization that even dates back further than the *Sai Yen* [Westerner's civilization]. We were writing books and poetry when they were still crawling around in caves!"

Old people converse with one another in Chinese, usually speaking variations of Cantonese—either *Sam Yap* [the third dialect], which originated in Namhoi, Punyu, and Shuntak districts of Kwangtung Province, or, most frequently, *Sze Yap* [the fourth dialect], from the Sunwei, Toishan, Hoiping, and Yanping districts of Kwangtung. The two dialects sound distinctly different when heard but are similar enough to be understood by those who speak one or the other because both originated in Canton, a city that serves as a language hub for the several dialect districts.

Old people voice a strong sense of accomplishment and happiness about their success in preserving the Chinese language in the Delta. An old woman reported:

The most important part of being Chinese is to say what you have to say in Chinese. I am very happy that my children have learned that. Even some of my grandchildren *gong ho Hon Yen Wah* [speak Chinese well]. It is so nice to hear them speak, almost like music to my ears. They show their respect to me when they visit by speaking Chinese instead of *Fan Wah* [English language]. They have not forgotten who they are.

Upon retirement (when they become too feeble to run a business), old people usually remain at home or move in with married children—after selling the store. They act as guardians and housekeepers for their children and grandchildren and take great pride in remaining useful to the family. Retirement involves a simple life. Old women cook, clean house, garden, and oversee grandchildren. They rise at dawn and retire at about 11:00 P.M. Mrs. Jong Gen, an old woman, outlined her routine activities to me:

> I don't sleep much, don't need to. I have been used to the long hours when we owned the store and so my life followed the rising and setting of the sun. Life is to be lived and not slept away like my children. I rise early in the morning just before the sun comes up. I take some time getting the house in order and then I cook breakfast for my son and his wife who must be at work around nine. I also cook for the children when they are in school. Later during the morning I work in the garden.[4] I cook lunch, wash the dishes and maybe some laundry around early afternoon. After that I take a short nap. Later in the afternoon I start cooking supper and serve it when everyone comes home from work. In the evening, I sew, mend clothes, and maybe watch some TV. Around eleven I go to bed and rest until the next morning.

Retired men "hang around" the family store and perform light tasks, wait on occasional customers, and offer business advice—all tasks which affirm their usefulness.

Old people and a few wives of businessmen practice ancient Chinese medicine. Younger groups, professionals and college students, consider old people's concoctions, home remedies, and folk beliefs and practices inadequate as compared with Western scientific medicine. Old people assert their herbal medicines are as good as modern Western medicine. Some individuals claim, for example, that Chinese teas "cure" the common cold and sore throats. Many experience the regret that their knowledge of traditional remedies will die with them. One old woman lamented: "My children believe in vitamins, but I believe in ginseng. It is a pity that the knowledge of many centuries of Chinese herbal medicine will go to the grave along with those who know the true value of life."[5]

[4] Many Chinese in the Delta grow in their own gardens traditional Southern vegetables such as eggplant, squash, tomatoes, and cucumbers, as well as traditional Chinese vegetables such as ginger, snow peas, kohlrabi, Chinese celery, bok choy, Chinese coriander, and *voo* [elephant ears].

[5] It should be mentioned that although many of these folk remedies are of Chinese origin, the Mississippi Chinese have assimilated many folk remedies indigenous to the South. My earlier research on health-care practices in the deep South suggests a cross-cultural dissemination of healing beliefs. See Julian B. Roebuck and Robert Quan, "Health-Care Practices in the Deep South: A Comparative Study," in *Marginal Medicine,* ed. Roy Wallis and Peter Morley (London: Peter Owen, 1976, New York: Free Press, 1977), pp. 141–161.

I found in visits to old people's kitchens that they emphasize the diet as a preventive health-care measure. Meals are prepared intentionally to balance *Yet* ["hot foods"] with *Leng* ["cold foods"][6] Soups made with seaweed or vegetables are usually considered "cold foods." Ginger, considered "hot," was used both as a seasoning and to balance out the "coldness" of soup. Fish was considered "cold food." Chicken was designated neutral, while duck was "hot." Certain vegetables and soups bring about a stability in the body resulting from an overabundance or imbalance of hot and cold foods. When soup fails, Chinese medicinal teas restore harmony to the body. Mrs. Wu Veen, who had practiced herbal healing in China (learned from her mother), maintained that a knowledge of Chinese herbal medicines was common among the older generation:

> Centuries have been spent by many Chinese doctors to refine herbal medicine. My mother taught me all she knew. She learned about herbs from her great-granduncle. Most of the old people here have some knowledge about herbs and teas. They had to because there were few doctors in China when we grew up. But you know, preventing health problems is much easier than trying to take care of them after you have it. I use my knowledge of nature to prepare balanced meals for my family. That way they don't need to take vitamins, but they still do anyway, they are like the *Lo Fan* [whites]. My herbs are the doctor's pills, even better and cheaper.

Another comment by an old woman, Mrs. Jaup Yek, illustrated the disagreement between the generations about Chinese medicine:

> Some of the professionals among us are pharmacists and medical students and they fail to see the good in Chinese healing. I don't think the new generation understands Chinese medicine—they would rather see a doctor even for *Yet Hee* [hot air or flatulence]. They think that I am *gu how naw* ["old skulls," that is, old-fashioned]. I guess this is because they are pharmacists and believe in modern medicine, hospitals, and specialists. They make it very clear to me that they are not interested in what I have to teach them about Chinese medicine, so the knowledge will die with me. This is so unfortunate. . . .

[6] The emphasis on a balance between hot and cold foods originates from the Chinese conception of harmony between, *Yin* [cold, dark, passive] and *Yang* [warm, light, active] forces, which operate throughout the universe.

19

I observed that respect and deference are extended to old people by way of titles and greetings. Elders are assigned titles on the basis of family position and age. I often did not know what to call a certain elder and had to ask someone. Responses to my question were expressed in the form of another question: "How old is your mother and father?" If the person whom I was addressing turned out to be younger than my mother, she was referred to as *Ah Seem* [aunt].[7] But if the woman was older than my mother, she was designated *Ah Mo* [elder aunt]. For males the same rule applied. A man younger than my father was referred to as *Ah Sook* [uncle], and one older than my father was *Ah Bok* [elder uncle]. Within the Chinese family, brothers and sisters have deference titles. For example, the eldest sister is referred to as *Ah Dee* and the eldest brother is called *Ah Goo*. On the other hand, the youngest sister is referred to as *Ah Moy,* and the youngest brother is called *Ah Hai.* Old people try to maintain a status system in the Chinese community based on age and respect by teaching deference titles to children and grandchildren.

Old people declared that they were reared with clear-cut guidelines about male and female sex roles. They claim that men are the leaders, providers, decision makers, and protectors, whereas women are guardians of the hearth. Women are expected to cook, clean, bring up the children, and teach them respect. They said their marriages were arranged and consummated in early adulthood and that this practice gave couples a long period of time to adjust to one another. Some old people are dismayed by the current generation's failure, in the view of their elders, to take marriage seriously. The aged lament the fact that young people have become Americanized and have been taught to regard partners in marriage as equals. This attitude, it is felt, weakens the decision-making process in the family. Old people resent young Chinese women who demonstrate independence about dating and marriage. An elderly

---

[7] "Aunt" in this case is a fictive kinship tie, because I was no blood relation to these people. On the other hand, my real aunt would be called *Ah Gwoo* instead of *Ah Seem.* Fictive kinships are found in all Chinese communities and are used to assign status to its members. This practice is supposed to insure deference and social order. One must have some kind of relationship title in the family group, for otherwise one is a stranger, and strangers are not acceptable.

woman registered the following complaint in speaking to her sister:

> I do not understand the modern generation who are educated and have money, yet they lack the common sense to do what is right . . ., to follow Chinese ways. These days the children are spoiled by their rich parents, who give them money and playthings rather than discipline and love. I don't like it even in my own family. Other old people I know say the same thing. When Chinese women marry the *Bok Guey* [whites], it hurts me deep inside, but that is the way it will be—but not the Chinese way. The traditional ties are loosening, but we all must accept it. It must be God's way.

Old people asked me frequently if I was married or had a girlfriend. They enjoy acting as go-betweens in arranging marriages. My encounter with Mrs. Guy Sil illustrates the point. We were sitting alone in her living room drinking Chinese tea one Sunday afternoon. On top of her television stood a graduation picture of a young woman. "That's my granddaughter," said Mrs. Guy Sil. "Isn't she beautiful?"

"Oh, yes! Of course, your granddaughter is very beautiful." The photograph showed a girl whose skin was quite light in comparison with the skins of the majority of Mississippi Chinese I had observed in the Delta. As I continued to look at the picture, Mrs. Guy Sil brought it closer, remarking, "She graduated from high school last year and is going to college at Ole Miss." She set the picture down near me.

"Are you married yet?" she asked politely.

"I'm still in school. This is my last year, and when I finish I plan on going back to San Francisco."

"Do you have a girlfriend?" I was familiar with the question from other, similar conversations. "If you don't have a girlfriend, I can introduce you to one. I know plenty of Chinese girls in the Delta who would make a pretty girlfriend and maybe even a wife. I found a good wife for my son last year. There are plenty of girls, but I know the good girls—you know, those who are *ho lai mau, ho nai, bok bok, den den* [good manners, beautiful, virtuous, faithful]. These girls are highly respected and come from good families. . . . A young man like you should get married." She spoke firmly. "I know someone that is perfect for you."

"Who do you have in mind?"

"Are you sure you are interested?"

I decided to profess interest, chiefly from curiosity about the extent of the old woman's diplomatic skills in this area. "Yes. Tell me her name."

"I cannot tell you her name because I don't think you are truly interested."

Clearly I was supposed to force her into revealing this information. I thought for a moment. "O.K., then, if you can't tell me her name, show me a picture of her."

"I cannot show you a picture. I don't have one," she said with obvious disappointment.

I do not know whether my relief was apparent. "Well, if you don't even have a picture of this girl, then we cannot do business today. Thank you for your interest."

The old woman withdrew, no doubt thinking as much of the many introductions she had made in the past as of her failure to trap me.

Old People at Work

The old people have made an economic niche for themselves as independent grocery merchants in black neighborhoods where neither white nor black merchants exist. They provide poor segregated blacks with convenient shopping facilities and credit. Many blacks do not have access to transportation necessary for shopping outside their isolated neighborhoods. Few white merchants will give them credit. Few blacks can finance grocery stores in their own areas. Whites are reluctant to operate grocery stores in neighborhoods where they would have to serve blacks and where poverty suggests that profits would be slim. The Chinese merchant thus fills an economic vacuum without antagonizing either blacks or whites. The blacks in fact accept their oriental neighbors as an asset, and the whites pose no objections. Many blacks feel more comfortable in Chinese stores than in white stores; Chinese merchants treat them with more civility than do white merchants, and blacks also feel more comfortable shopping in their own neighborhoods.

Whites are frequently discriminatory and openly disapprove of the way blacks talk, act, and dress. As one old shopkeeper explained:

> The *Lo Mok*[8] couldn't always go cross town to shop. Many had no cars. They couldn't get much credit from the white man, neither. They felt at home wid us because we didn't bother them about the way they dressed or acted. We give them respect. They didn't have to worry 'bout no white man neither, 'cause few white people come in. They needed us. We needed them. It twas a good deal all the way round.

Old people showed themselves to be hard-working, frugal business people. They open their grocery stores at seven in the morning and close between six and ten at night. They sell a wide assortment of items, including staples, canned goods, bottled drinks, fast foods, fruits, vegetables, tobacco, cigarettes, cosmetics, and some luxury items. The U.S. Food Stamp Program provides large profits for these general stores. In addition to tending the store, the merchants spend much time talking to customers, salesmen, clerks, and wholesalers. One old woman told me:

> We worked in the store to survive because when we first came over, we didn't have a nickel. We built the business from the bottom up, always saving money—not for ourselves, but for our children. We didn't want them to have to work long hard hours like us in this business. You see, with an education, at least people can go places in the world. I don't speak much English myself, but my children do. With that knowledge, they don't have to be like me, opeining up the store early in the morning and closing late at night, taking a few nickels and dimes from the *Lo Mok* [blacks].

Old people claim to perform important economic and social functions within the local community. One grocery store owner commented:

[8] Throughout this study several Chinese words for blacks appear. These terms may be literally translated as follows: *Lo Mok* [dark ink]; *Hok Guey* [black ghosts or devils]; and less formally: *Chi-han* [briquette]; *gnu-keem* [black swan gizzard]. It should be kept in mind that words denoting blacks are social constructions by the Chinese people. Each Chinese individual creates his own, for example, on one occasion I heard a Chinese merchant refer to blacks as *see yu guy* [soy sauce chicken]. This designation seemed to be a friendly and humorous expression, as opposed to *Hok Guey,* or "black ghosts."

TING AND FATHER Joe Ting's father, Joe Guay (seated next to Ting), bought the business from his brother, Joe King, in 1926. The store sold general merchandise, cattle feed as well as Chinese art objects, clothes, groceries, and herbs until WWII began. Chinese groceries were sold to Chinese retail grocers in nearby Southern states.
Courtesy of the Joe Ting Collection

I could have sold the store a long time ago and made a profit to retire. But what's the use, my customers are very dear to me. Many have traded with me since the other stores closed down. Like Mr. Lo Moon across the street. He got too old to work, and his wife passed away about seven years ago. You know, he had nothing to do, so he sold the store, packed up, and went to live with his son in Houston, Texas. All of my customers are very nice to me. They are old, too, and like to come by and talk once in a while. One old-time customer said to me yesterday: "Miz Pau, don't close up the store, because then I won't have anyone to talk to. All my children have moved away. Oh, Mrs. White is such a nice lady. Most of my customers are that way—we're all friends."

Old people manage to be cordial as well as efficient in dealing with black and white customers. They get along well with blacks and whites. Therefore they prosper in business. I witnessed the following dialogue, between Mr. Geem Lung, lifelong owner of a grocery store that formerly belonged to his father, and Mr. Calhoun, an old black customer. Mr. Calhoun, as was his habit, entered and purchased a tin of Prince Albert tobacco and some cigarette papers. Mr. Geem Lung introduced me to him with great warmth: "Mr. Quan and I, Leroy, we was talking about the '27 flood and how we made it through. I know you remember those times well."

"Sho do . . . Them was hard days. . . . I remember Mr. Lung [addressing me], bless his soul, fed me and a lot of my family. . . . 'Course, we all helped each other out a lot in them days. Credit —I paid up when I could. They was patient."

Mr. Geem Lung quickly added, "It was hard for all of us who had big families to have enough to eat."

Mr. Calhoun nodded agreement. "Uh huh. Cornbread and buttermilk, we sho did eat a lot of that."

Looking at Mr. Calhoun, I asked: "What? No rice?" "Oh, yes." Mr. Geem Lung replied. "Always rice." Later, speaking with me, he observed: "My customers are my friends, they always have been. They know who I am and I know who they are. Being *Hon Yen* [Chinese] doesn't mean that you don't find out pretty quick what is what about everybody. *Lo Mok* [blacks] or *Lo Fan* [whites] or *Hon Yen*, it doesn't make any difference in a small town. I've known almost all of my customers for many years. This store is my home. . . ." Old people recalled the difficult times brought on by the 1927 flood and later the depression years. However, they maintained that most businesses were not ruined by the flood. Some in fact found an opportunity to make even more money. One old man told me:

> It was the best year we had. You see, our store was right next to the levee.... all the refugees camped on top of the levee, so anything we could cook and take out to sell, they bought it. Sure, I even remember the water mark. It was about three foot high. We raised everything up to the second story and carried on as usual. Some of the other Chinese merchants had to be evacuated, but after the flood was over, none of them had any casualties or problems. They all come back all right.

The elderly businessmen recalled that during the depression Chinese merchants survived by their thriftiness and readiness to help each other. One old merchant noted:

> The depression was no particular problem to the Chinese businessmen. We always save our money and pay our debt. So without a debt no matter the depression, we do business. Well, let's say a loaf of bread—today it costs twenty cents, depression tomorrow costs ten cents. I sell for ten cents. I buy another one for eight cents. I still make two pennies. But if you owe someone money, and you sell at ten cents, you be sunk. We helped each other too and didn't pay no interest when we paid it back.

During the first half of the twentieth century many of the Chinese knew too little English to do business with people in the outside world. To cope with the problem they founded an informal mutual protection association. As one elderly grocer said:

> We businessmen always helped each other out, like in a family. One person would look after the other, and then nobody failed. We make sure that debts were paid back to keep the Chinese credit rating high. Back in those times you didn't see any Chinese filing bankruptcy. You see, what one person did affected the whole group. But in the sixties it began changing . . ., too many people being Americanized. It's not like what it used to be.

I had an opportunity one afternoon to talk with one old woman who still worked at her son's grocery store. Mrs. Geem Hao and I sat in the back of the store, which at one time had been the living quarters for all the family. After the family had made a fortune in the grocery business (in a black neighbor-

A majority of the Mississippi Delta Chinese own and operate small grocery stores in black neighborhoods. Many once lived behind their stores out of convenience and to preclude any potential conflicts that might arise with whites resisting encroachment in their neighborhoods.

hood), she told me, she and her son had built a large expensive house in a neighborhood where other successful Chinese merchants and some white professionals lived. Nevertheless, in her eyes the back of the store was still "home" and would always be.

We came here to *Nam Fong* [the South] and lived in *Hok Guy Fao* [black neighborhood] and have run this store for a long time. You can tell by the cement walls of the store that we came here to stay and to make money. We came to make a living here. Who else would want to live in this place? The *Bok Guey* [whites] are too

27

proud to live in this place and the *Hok Guey* [blacks] cannot go anywhere. So that just leaves the *Hon Yen* [Chinese], and we do the best we can.

I said, "Geem Hao Seem, why don't you take it easy in your old age . . .?"

"I don't do much work any more. Just keep busy . . . a little here . . ., a little there," she replied.

"Let your young son and his wife do the work."

She sighed. "They work hard, too. This store is theirs now, not mine any more. It was mine and my husband's for twenty-five years . . ., long enough, now time to let the young minds and the strong arms take over."

"Twenty-five years is a long time in Mississippi. . . ." She began to talk more while serving me Chinese tea.

> Yes, it is better for me. [My son] is a good businessman and takes good care of the bookkeeping. I draw social security now and take what little money I need. In this small town there is nowhere to spend money, and I would not spend my money anyway . . . might need it some day. So you just make it and save it—you know, put it in a coffee can so it won't burn and stick it in the ground or something. Hide it. The old people do not believe in banks, never did. You know about history. I just don't want the government to rob me of my precious savings. I won't live much longer—just long enough to help my children and grandchildren through . . ., you know, give them an education. They cannot go to college without money, so you see why I keep all my money a secret.

Many old people still operate grocery stores and still manage to sustain long working hours. If they are not waiting on customers at the front or behind the counter, they stack merchandise, clean-up, cut meat, bag chickens, write bills, and handle invoices. They talk to wholesalers and delivery men, check in new stock, and gather information about other grocery stores when they are not preoccupied with other tasks. One old-time store owner, Mr. Fut Lok, described to me his activities on a typical day.

> Business starts around seven in the morning when my wife and I open the store. Farmers and farm workers come in to buy small items like doughnuts and soft drinks. Then there is a slack period around nine to ten. That's when the *men bow guey* [breadmen] and the *gnow ni guey* [milkmen] arrive. I chat with them and get

some of the news about other stores and what is going on around the Delta. Around ten to ten thirty some of the *gon hen guey* [farmers] who drive around all day in their trucks, you know, the old ones who ain't got nothing to do, come in for an apple pie and some pop to wash it down. Some even come in and sit on the milk crate and watch their favorite TV program. Those guys got time to spend, because their boys do all the work now—they've retired. So around eleven the workers and the *Lo Mok* [blacks] come drifting in to buy sandwiches and lunch meat like bologna and souse meat. It gets really busy then. Also, you got a lot of young kids coming in to buy candy and old *Lo Moks* [blacks] from around town who buy most of their groceries. It gets so busy that my wife has to come out to the front and wait on customers.

About one, I go to the back and eat lunch. Then, when I'm finished, my wife eats and I run the front. Then when nobody's around I take a nap. The trucks usually come in around three or three-thirty, so my wife wakes me up and I go to check in the stock. Business is sometimes like a flood—everybody all at once. And then sometimes it is just a trickle. Around five business steps up because everyone is getting off work. They stop by the store to pick up things to eat for supper. When the sun goes down things get slow and we close around eight-thirty. That's when I relax, eat supper, watch a little TV, maybe read the newspaper and then "hit the sack." I do this six days a week all year around. I'm about worn out telling you all this. Let's get something cold to drink. You want a beer? Have something. . . .

I learned that every other night in most grocery stores the money taken in is counted, bills are sorted, change is rolled, and food stamps are certified "For Deposit Only" with the store's bank account number. Old people told me that this money is taken to the bank the following morning and deposited. One store owner's description of how he treated money indicated the frugality characteristic of the Chinese:

> Sure, I like to make money, and with Uncle Sam's food stamp program, these coupons are as good as the real stuff [pointing to the money laid out in piles on the table]. I just stamp them like this [showing me] and take 'em down to the bank. I go to the bank about three times a week, but not to make a withdrawal like the *Lo Fan* [whites], but a deposit—a big deposit. This is how I can afford to give each of my children a car when they graduate from school.

Old store owners confided to me that white middle-class customers were treated more respectfully and were given more attention than black customers. I noted that white customers appeared to be convivial and talkative. Conversation with whites, however, generally involved topics no more profound than the weather and crops. Merchants called all white customers Mr. and Mrs. even when they were not present. On the other hand, whites greet Chinese by their first names or initials. By the familiar and condescending manner in which they talk to the store owners, white customers make it very clear that they feel themselves superior to the merchants. Sincere affection and equalitarian familiarity in the South are expressed only with relatives and close friends. Still, as one Chinese shopkeeper remarked, "I don't care what they call me just as long as they bring me the money."

Chinese merchants and black customers address each other by Mr., Miss, Mrs., especially those blacks who have earned the respect of other blacks in the Delta. As one merchant explained, "That way we don't make the white man angry, and we make the *Lo Mok* happy."

Chinese merchants exercise a ploy of "trading," or serial buying and selling, with blacks but never with whites. Blacks are encouraged to buy and pay for one item at a time. Such an arrangement permits blacks to display buying power and the merchant to earn more money from them by suggesting a series of purchases. The following encounter illustrates the practice.

A black man entered, walked to the counter, and said, "Give me a sixpack of Schlitz and some hot sausage." After he spoke he leaned against the counter to see who else was in the store.

Mr. Fah Tong peered into the meat case. "How much do you want?"

"Give me two dollar worth."

The shopkeeper placed a handful of sausages on a piece of butcher paper and turned to the scale directly behind him. Having wrapped the meat, Mr. Fah Tong reached for the beer in the next case and returned to the counter to sack everything. When he had done so he pushed the bag of groceries to the center of the counter and said, "Four twenty-five."

The customer shook his head and produced a five-dollar bill, which he tossed on the counter nonchalantly. Mr. Fah Tong placed the money on the ledge of the cash register and pulled out two quarters, two dimes, and a nickel. He slapped the change against the top of the counter and removed his hand.[9]

"Anything else?"

The customer picked up his change one coin at a time. When he finished, he asked for a package of Kool cigarettes.

Mr. Fah Tong placed the cigarettes on the counter. "Fifty cents. Anything else?"

The customer paid again but still looked around. Mr. Fah Tong sensed that he had more money to spend. After all, five dollars on a weekday meant plenty of money. Behind the counter an assortment of items could be seen: combs, brushes, handkerchiefs, wristwatch bands, health-care products, fishing hooks, dog collars, and so forth. The man finally fixed his eyes on a pair of sunglasses. "Let me see them shades."

Mr. Fah Tong replied: "Oh, you don't need that. Only white people wear those things."

"How much?"

"Three fifty."

Silence.

"O.K., gimme them." The customer tried them on for size and removed another five-dollar bill from his wallet. Then, picking up his change quickly, he grabbed the sack of groceries and hastened out the door.

The preceding episode shows how Chinese store owners take advantage of blacks' trading practices and encourage impulse buying. Merchants also place low-cost items in full view near the cash register. Customers are thus encouraged to spend their small change before leaving the store.

Old Chinese grocers are also adroit at managing black children, as the next case indicates. A young black girl purchased a loaf of bread with a one-dollar food coupon. The grocer hesitated in returning a stamped note for the change due and said, "O.K, you have five cents and you can pick out two pieces of bubble gum or candy or cookies if you want." The little girl gazed at the variety of items lining the counter above her head.

[9] Mr. Fah Tong, like many other Chinese merchants, operates on a cash basis and extends credit only to trustworthy blacks he has known for a long time. He said that breaking up change is a strategy by which he encourages more trading —"Blacks think they are richer when they see more change on the counter."

She pointed at the vanilla sandwich cookies sitting in a jar. The merchant deftly slipped two cookies into a small paper bag and handed it to the young customer.

After this sale, the grocer told me, "All of the black kids usually buy some cookies or candy before leaving the store." He explained that mothers ordinarily allow children to spend the remaining change as they please after they have run an errand.

Soon thereafter two other black youngsters walked into the store and purchased three cookies for five cents. After paying for the merchandise, the children went outside to eat their treat. Later, one of the two girls walked back in and asked the merchant, "How come I only got two cookies and the other girl got three?"

The merchant leaned over the counter and answered, "Cause your cookies got more filling in 'em." The little girl seemed satisfied with the answer and walked out.

Old People at Church

Old people throughout the Delta are committed Christians and church members. They make a profession of faith in Jesus Christ and say they have been "saved by the blood of the Lamb." Most take an active part in church programs. Many were religious leaders in the community when the Chinese first sought acceptance by whites in the Delta. They foresaw that becoming Christian was the first necessary step toward the goal. They also found that they could learn the English language by means of church services, religious instruction, and Bible readings. The old people act as moral guides and Christian teachers, and they attain spiritual and economic security through hard work, religious devotion, and self-sacrifice.

Although some individuals combined traditional Chinese Buddhist beliefs and customs with Christianity, only a few non-Christians practiced outright ancestor worship. Chinese non-Christians often "witness to Jesus" when dying so that they can be given a Christian burial. Younger members of the family usually demand Christian rites. Chinese funerals follow the American rather than the traditional Chinese pattern, with the result that death and dying become a part of the Americaniza-

CHINESE BAPTIST CHURCH The Chinese Baptist Church of Cleveland, Mississippi, was built in 1957 and serves Chinese in other small towns within a radius of forty miles. An education building and the fellowship hall were added in 1976.

These Chinese Christians worship together every Sunday afternoon at 2 P.M. Old people act as moral guides and Christian teachers to the young. Chinese women spend time reading the Bible and organizing business and social affairs of the church.

33

tion process. One old woman described her need to bury her husband a Christian:

> My family are all Christians and have been baptized in the church. My husband wouldn't, though. He never cared much about religion, but he was a good provider for the family. When he was dying, it made us feel better that he witnessed to Jesus just before he passed away. The preacher was there at his deathbed. We all felt better that he had a Christian burial. All of us who are saved will be together in heaven when the day comes.... that is what the Bible says, and we believe it.

I focused on the Chinese Baptist Church of Cleveland, which serves Chinese in other small towns within a forty-mile radius including Greenwood, because the Mississippi Chinese consider it to be the established main church—and because other Chinese missions follow the same program. Most old people belong to this church and attend regular Sunday afternoon services. The preacher, a Chinese Baptist minister hired from outside the area, and a few dedicated old men and women, the founders and deacons, are recognized leaders. The church, a red brick structure built in 1957, stands next to the Chinese Mission School on Highway 8 in Cleveland. New additions were made in 1976, including an education building and a fellowship hall. The parsonage is located directly behind the church on East Main Street in what is now a working-class Chinese neighborhood.

The church opens into a foyer. A set of double swinging doors leads to the sanctuary, where ten oak pews fixed on each side of a carpeted aisle face the pulpit. Although the building has a seating capacity of two hundred, regular attendance is about thirty each Sunday. Approximately twelve feet behind the pulpit are several choir chairs. At stage left is a built-in baptismal pool shrouded by a dark velvet curtain. A piano sits at ground level nearby.

Old people walk or travel to the church in cars driven by their children or relatives. Some old men drive cars, but most old women have never learned to drive. Worship services are held at two o'clock in the afternoon, in keeping with store hours (grocery stores open on Sundays at eight in the morning and business is usually slow between two and four o'clock, picking

34

up again around five). One old woman told me her Sunday schedule:

> On Sunday morning I open up the store at eight with one of my boys. Around one we eat dinner. I fix the dinner and my boy watches the front and takes care of customers. At two we close up for a couple of hours and he drives me to church. Around three thirty church is over, and he takes me back to the store and work until nine, when we close up and go home. Sunday is not a real busy day, not like Friday or Saturday, when the *Lo Mok* [blacks] get paid and spend their money. Then we have to work real hard. They come in to buy groceries and settle up their bills.

Old people sit in pews at stage right, alongside middle-aged married couples. Occasionally young married couples sit with them. College students and young people sit together on the left side of the aisle. The Chinese Baptist minister and the deacons conduct the services. The form and content of the presentation are traditional Southern Baptist. Prayers, Scripture readings, recitations, and the sermon are given in Chinese and English. Hymns are sung in English.

The preacher delivers the sermon in *Sam Yap* [third dialect of Cantonese] and clarifies certain portions of the presentation in English. A few church members complained to me that the preacher should speak in *Sze Yap* [fourth dialect], one that all the church members understand and speak at home. One person said:

> I speak and understand *Sze Yap* because most of the Chinese here in the Delta communicate in that dialect. We were raised that way. The young people may not speak Chinese very well, but they understand it. The preacher uses a formal Cantonese dialect, *Sam Yap*, and most of us have a hard time following him. It just seems to make more sense if he spoke our dialect. Now, sometimes, one of the deacons will deliver a message in *Sze Yap*, and I think all of us understand it better. It must be hard for the younger generation to understand Chinese because they don't get much exposure to it—not as much as I did, anyway. Their parents speak more English to them than Chinese, so what do you expect? Their children are going to forget how to speak Chinese. It's still good that Chinese is spoken here at the church so the old people can understand the teachings of Christ.

Old people often act as lay missionaries in the Delta and "witness" and "testify to others. They devote much time to reading and translating the Bible into Chinese. Some individuals told me that an undying Christian faith had enabled them to perform strong leadership roles during the early years of the Chinese community when the Chinese worked hard to rid themselves of the image of being "colored." (The facts seem to indicate, however, that the pressure to become Christians preceded Christian faith.) One old woman talked to me about the pressing need of the Chinese to become Christians:

> In 1925 there were not too many Chinese in the Delta. Mrs. Leong's mother-in-law., Hoo Shee Leong, came to the Delta in 1913. Seid Chun Wah was also another woman around at that time. The oldest living Chinese woman in the Delta is Doy Lee Moo. She's eighty years old. Well, there were maybe eleven Chinese families at that time. Then Dr. Eavenson came back from China and started a mission for us in the First Baptist Church. You know, he was a missionary back in China. So the whites asked us to go to church, and some even came and picked us up. So we went and became Christians. That's when we became accepted in the community and figured out that the Caucasians would talk about us living like that. We wanted our children to go to white schools and learn how to read and write. So we went to church and the *Bok Guey* [whites] saw us as okay. We had to show them we were Chinese, not colored.

As this account indicates, the early Delta Chinese felt pressure in three significant areas: (1) they had to become Christians in order to be accepted by the white community; (2) they had to learn English in order to adjust and survive; (3) they had to disassociate themselves from blacks in order to be accepted by the white power structure as a separate Chinese ethnic group. The probable alternative was eventual amalgamation with blacks.

Old people noted that the Baptist religion had intrigued them in part because of the prohibition on drinking, smoking, and gambling. They say that the similarity of the Christian religion to Chinese religion made it easier for them to convert. One old woman said: "The Baptist religion is very much like Chinese religious way of thinking. You know; no smoking, drinking, and gambling. Also, the Baptists believed in keeping the family close together, like Chinese families do. So we converted over to the Baptist way of thinking pretty easy. It was much like the Chinese way we were taught at home." Probably a more significant but less proclaimed reason for becoming Christian relates to the surrounding pervasive Christian culture and the orthodoxy of the white power structure. As one old man remarked, "It's hard to be a Buddhist in a Christian sea."

Old people taught their children to be Christians, to leave other people alone, and to obey parents and the law. As one old woman explained:

> We old people try to set an example for the rest of the Chinese community by showing our faith and right actions. We take great pride in our church and our young children who attend it. They have learned to stay out of trouble with the law by placing their faith in their family and church. We always told our children not to bother nobody. We have provided our children with ways of right action. To do what is right and to be able to live with their decisions and not bring dishonor to themselves or their family. I think we have been very successful Christian teachers. You do not find Chinese breaking the law here—these children stay out of trouble. These young people are taught discipline and to do what is right. We old people have seen to that. . . .

Old people avoid conflict among themselves and with others and focus attention on economic goals. As one old man reported: "The Chinese had to work long hours and give up any time to relax and take it easy. They had big families to feed, so they tried to get along with everyone. They saved their money and made themselves successful. The recipe for success is honesty, hard work, and saving money, and that is why everyone respects the Chinese." A few old people reported to me that some Delta Chinese blended Chinese religious customs with Christian beliefs and practices and that a few people continued to practice ancestor worship. When I interviewed a Christian minister, however, he claimed that such observances were a thing of the past. "When the Chinese first came to the Delta, their religious background was not clear. I think they used to practice it until they became Christians. But now the only ones practicing ancestor worship are the non-Christians."

"How do these people who follow ancestor worship pay tribute to the dead?"

"Some of them go to the graveyard and burn incense and pray. Others take meat and worship. Most, though, don't practice ancestor worship like they do in San Francisco. They just put flowers on the grave and say a prayer. This is called 'ancestor respect.'"

One old man told me about the Chinese cemetery in Greenville. His account shows how burial practices are linked with race relations of the living.

The Chinese cemetery in Greenville was started in 1928, a year after Charles Lindbergh crossed the Atlantic. There was a Chinese man named Seto and he wanted to fly across the Pacific. He even showed us a picture with him standing next to Lindbergh and the plane. I don't know how he got that picture, but all the Chinese merchants helped Seto to raise $2,200 to buy the plane. Later we find out that he never bought it, so we kept the money and bought the cemetery. Back when the Chinese first settled, they isolated themselves from everyone. The Chinese is a strange people. They think their way is better. Well, the Chinese ran into difficulties with whites who wouldn't let them use the *Bok Guey fun cheng* [white graveyard]. And the Chinese didn't want to be buried with the *Lo Mok* [blacks] 'cause we was a different people, so we all got the Chinese cemetery started.

Another elderly member of the Chinese Cemetery Committee in Greenville told of the return of Chinese bodies to China and indicated that racial discrimination persisted after death. The dead in such cases are symbols of the living.

We used to ship the bones back to China until 1941—that's when the war interrupted it. We'd ship the bodies back to a Hong Kong warehouse and they would take it back to the village in China. There were eight of us on the cemetery committee, and we were responsibile for getting everything arranged. We'd get the health department to okay it, get a nice box, and have the funeral home come and dig up the body. Most of the Chinese funerals were handled by Wells Funeral Home in Greenville. You see, the Chinese cemetery is free. You just pay fifty dollars for maintenance. Most Chinese are still buried there because the whites charge five to six thousand dollars for the funeral and plot. And they don't want us anyway. Chinese don't pay for the plot—it's cheaper, you see.[10]

[10]In the Chinese view of filial piety and cultural continuity, the life of mankind is considered an unbroken continuum of the dead, the living, and the yet unborn; by paying homage to the spirits of ancestors, the Chinese reaffirm the eternal life of mankind. Honor is brought to both the individual and the family as well as to descendants. For a detailed description of the process entailed in preparing the bones for reburial at a propitious site, see Valentine R. Burkhardt, *Chinese Creeds and Customs* (Hong Kong: South China Morning Post, 1954).

CHINESE CEMETERY IN GREENVILLE The Chinese Cemetery in Greenville, Mississippi, was started in 1928 by local Chinese businessmen who wanted a burial place for the Chinese. During that time, segregation excluded Chinese from white cemeteries and the Chinese did not wish to share life after death with blacks in their cemeteries.

A few people cling to some Buddhist beliefs, although they are aware that some tenets of their religion are being transformed, for example, ancestor worship. Younger generation members often refer to ancestor worship as "ancestor respect," a phrase by which they tacitly acknowledge the Christian belief that "you shall have no other gods before me." By such redefinition of traditional Chinese beliefs and practices, the Mississippi Chinese have rendered them more compatible with Baptist Christianity. It remains true, however, that Delta Chinese Christians differ somewhat in their belief systems from white Christians. The response of an elderly Chinese woman to her granddaughter about a proposed trip to a distant state soon after a death in the immediate family demonstrates the persistence of the Chinese religious way. "It is wrong to dishonor your ancestors so soon after they have passed on. You must remain for one month to pay your respects and mourn. Unnecessary travel is unthinkable. That is the Way...." The continued observance of such customs is open to question, however. The granddaughter reluctantly agreed to postpone her trip until the specified period had elapsed, but she later confided to me her anger. "That old woman is crazy with her old superstitions. I have never heard of this one-month thing. I think she made it up so I couldn't leave. You know a lot of those old ladies think the same way. . . . death is some big deal for them. They believe in evil spirits that will come back and haunt you and everything. That's a bunch of bull."

Old People at Leisure

Old people's work precludes many recreational activities. Work and recreation are often intermixed because the residence and the work site are one and the same place. Old people share their leisure time with the family. Some elderly Chinese go fishing. They look forward to American and Chinese holidays: the Chinese New Year, the Harvest Moon, Easter, Thanksgiving, Christmas, and birthdays—times when they reunite with friends and family members. Old people proclaim their success, talk about hopes for their children and grandchildren, and tell themselves and others during holidays that they are somebody.

Old people play the role of cook, host, and hostess during festive occasions. Proud of their cooking talent, they prepare many Cantonese dishes at holiday time. They procure the necessary ingredients from their grocery stores and from commercial sources in Chicago, Los Angeles, and San Francisco. They have Chinese lucky money, *Lee Shee,* wrapped in red envelopes for children during the Chinese New Year and the Harvest Moon. The envelopes are designed in gold signifying happiness and prosperity. Old women bake special moon cakes during the Harvest Moon.

Chinese holidays also give the old women a chance to show their cooking skills. *Tay Doy* [tea pastries] and *Char sil bow* [pork buns] are made to accompany large sumptuous meals. Relatives are invited from all over the Delta. Although old people rarely leave home, they occasionally attend a wedding or a banquet. Friends and relatives come to visit and pay their respects. Old people expect deference as a reward for long years of hard work. One old man indicated the joy derived from family life: "We don't have time to play. We must be serious in order to survive. . . . history has taught us that. But we get great pleasure from our family. . . . that is the center of our attention."

Most of the old people's recreational activities take place in the home. I was once invited to a birthday party hosted by an elderly couple, Mr. and Mrs. Fah Tong. Thirty people were present, including Mr. and Mrs. Fah Tong's children, grandchildren, relatives on both sides of the family, in-laws, and close friends. Knots of people stood in the living room, halls, dining room, and kitchen. I was introduced to many of the guests in English and was led by a friend to a large dining table for a drink of lemonade, soda pop, or iced tea. Chinese and American food was spread out buffet style on several tables.

I met the honored old couple in the kitchen and at an opportune time said to them in Cantonese: "I am very honored to be invited here to celebrate Mr. Fah Tong's sixty-fifth birthday. I want to wish you and your family peace, prosperity, and longevity and much social security!" Everyone chuckled. I identified some of the people who were present from pictures on the living-room wall.

In the course of the party the nature of a number of conversations under way in English and Cantonese throughout the room prompted me to ask a friend nearby why Chinese always talked about money.

"Oh," she replied, putting her plate down, "that's a subject of common interest because they never had any money before and over the years they've sacked away quite a bit of it."

"But what do they spend it on? Not on new furniture or a new house."

"The Chinese spend it on cars. . . . It's a big status symbol, owning a Buick." I prodded her for further information. "Well, the Chinese also invest in real estate, some of which they rent out, like houses, laundries, and hotels to the blacks. A few merchants buy property in hopes of building a home on it someday."

At this point Mr. Fah Tong approached.

"Just takes hard work," he said, breaking into the conversation. "Most of the Chinese I know are respected because the *Bok Guey* [whites] and the *Lo Mok* [blacks] know we have money. You don't find us on any welfare, do you? The old people came up hard during rough times. Because of that the younger ones have it easier. So money represents to us freedom: we're free to buy"—he moved in closer and lowered his voice —"any goddamn thing we want. Money talks in these small towns. People treat you right and stay off your back because they know in the back of their minds that you've got it, but they don't know how much—so I just let them keep guessing. . . ."

I asked, "What did the old people do for recreation back in the old days?"

Mr. Fah Tong then explained the origins of the Ong Leng Merchants Association, a Chinese tong:

> In 1930 men didn't have their wives here and there were few Chinese women. On Sunday there was no place to go. The Ong Leng tong from St. Louis came down to organize a tong in Greenville. You know, gambling, so the Chinese could get together and have a little fun. Only a few went to church, but most of us tired of working all the time. But later on the tong got out of hand. Some of the Chinese tried to blackmail local merchants. See, at that time the tong was made up of small families with the same surname (Seid, Hong, Lee). They tried to enforce the same tong law as in St. Louis and Chicago. Like, within certain distance you

couldn't organize another grocery store. We were the biggest family, and we didn't like it when they sent a threatening letter to us . . ., if you don't do this and that, you will face the consequences. I interpreted the letter to the sheriff, and two tong people got picked up. So the tong in St. Louis sent a big shot out here with the same last name as our family to deal with the trouble with the tong. The tong got plenty of money and you are doing business. He told us that the best way to eliminate them is to all get together and join them and they will lose their power anyway. Well, he was right, the more people join, the more voice. Well, the tong got disbanded around 1948–49 because the women came over. Merchants didn't have the time to visit anymore. The tong started in 1936 and lasted until 1949, after the Exclusion Act was repealed in 1943.

The conversation with Mr. Fah Tong indicated to me, among other things, that old people have become capitalists and are Americanized to a great extent.

Old People in the Triethnic Community

In their lifetimes the old people have succeeded in gaining respect and acceptance from both whites and blacks as a third ethnic group, the Mississippi Delta Chinese. Now they are economically successful, but they still remain independent, neutral, and apolitical in biracial matters. "We Chinese just wanted to make it in the Delta," one old man told me. "We didn't try to bother nobody. We just wanted to make a living and to be accepted, that's all. The first generation didn't want to be black, 'colored,' or white."
Mr. Sil Seem said:

I first came over when I was ten years old. I worked for my uncle in his store in the Delta. I saved money and go back to China and got married. I come back three years later and work, save money and send back to my family in China. I do this for about two years because I make pretty good money here. Then I go back again and bring family over here. Most of the other old people will tell you same story. We all did that. We stick together, work, and don't bother nobody. We don't mix with nobody, we keep our mouth shut, no talk, just work. Now we talk with other Chinese when we see them to find out what they do. But then, not many Chinese at that time. We don't want to become *Bok Guey* [whites] and we sure don't want to become "colored" like the *Hok Guey* [blacks],

43

no sir, those people were treated worse than dogs. We don't want that to happen to us anyhow, anywhere, anyway. We just want to be ourselves, *Hon Yen* [Chinese].

Still another old man described the rules that Chinese lived by in "the early days" to stay out of trouble and survive.

The Chinese is a funny people. As a whole they tend to their own business. And what happened, they don't care. That's the reason they stayed out of trouble, see. They go butting in this fellow's business. . . . first thing you know, somebody got killed or something another. My mother always told us children, when somebody do that, don't say nothing, don't you say you saw it, just turn your head and walk. Don't let them catch you. You witness and you're dead! They gonna get you if you witness. You witness against the other fellow, you dead. He gonna kill you. That's why we always mind our own business. That's the way we stayed out of trouble with blacks and whites and lived to be old.

Old people claimed they established and maintained a Chinese Delta community by working industriously and accepting the race relations of blacks and whites. They became economically self-sufficient, practiced endogamy, avoided racial conflict, and accepted Christianity. One elderly woman outlined the historical development of the Chinese community and shed some light on attitudes toward interracial marriage (taboo among the Mississippi Chinese).[11]

When there was just a few of us in the Delta there wasn't much problem with the Chinese. There was just a few Chinese men who took *Lo Mok* wives, but we didn't have anything to do with them, that's all. In our tradition we don't go for mixed marriages, but on account of the Exclusion Act many Chinese men couldn't bring their wives over. Later on the Chinese community started growing. We started families and some of the immigrants brought their half-grown children over. That's when the *Lo Fan* [whites] began to take notice. The Baptists was interested in Chinese. Methodist never was. They think they was a better class. We went to church and got converted to become Christians. We gave them lots of money, and they saw to it that we was treated different from the *Lo Mok*. I mean, they saw to it that we had to be a separate group of our own.

[11]Though we know from Loewen that interracial marriage with blacks seldom occurred and that the progeny from such marriages was probably limited, we know little about miscegenation among the Chinese and blacks.

Old people remembered racial discrimination as a local matter and stated that the extent of racial segregation varied from one Delta town to another. Social and institutional discrimination was at a minimum in small towns with only a few Chinese families. On the other hand, in large towns (for example, Cleveland and Greenville) where the Chinese were more concentrated, they were often the victims of prejudice and discrimination. One episode involving a Chinese man from Shaw, Mississippi, triggered the enforcement of segregation laws in Greenville. An elderly man told me about the case.

> Around 1912 to 1915, I don't remember exactly, a Chinese man named Quon took ill and went to Kings Daughter Hospital in Greenville. You see, there was two Kings Daughter hospitals. One was white and located on Arnold Street, and the other was colored, located on Alexander Street. Both were private. Quon went to the white hospital—those were the only two hospitals around at that time, and they were private. A colored woman came to see her husband at the hospital. You know, she gave his name and everything. The whites kicked them out! From that time on, things got worse, and the Chinese couldn't even get a haircut sometimes. Even at the Italian barbershop!

Old people recalled no law which prevented them from attending a white church, though there was a law which prevented them from going to white schools. The Mississippi Constitution of 1890 specified that separate schools were to be maintained for children of the white and colored races, and because Chinese were not considered white, they fell under the heading of the "colored races."[12] Therefore the Chinese faced the problem of educating their children. They did not want them to go to black schools for three reasons: (1) as Chinese they did not accept the white man's designation of them as "colored," (2) the black schools were inferior to the white schools, (3) they did not wish to be assimilated (or amalgamated) into the black culture or race. One old woman related the educational situation in the mid-1920s:

> By law the Chinese weren't allowed to go to the *Bok Guey* [white] schools, but because there weren't many Chinese families back then, some went anyway. If you lived in a small town and you

12Loewen, *The Mississippi Chinese*, pp. 64–69.

mixed with the *Bok Guey*, was good friends with them, they would let the Chinese go to their schools 'cause they don't know no better. But as soon as someone objected on account of the law, they had to get rid of them. For example, if somebody said she's colored, she's Chinese, then you would have to be dismissed. You see, that's what happened to Mrs. Gong Lum. She was a very educated lady from Hong Kong, and she got very angry with the Rosedale School board because they kicked her children, Berda and Martha, out of the *Bok Guey* school. Somebody must have objected because at that time I don't think Rosedale allowed the Chinese in their school. Anyway, she tried to bring a lawsuit to make them let her children go to school. She thought she could bluff them, and it didn't go. I know other Chinese who went to the *Bok Guey* school up in Marks, Dublin, Shelby—up there. They didn't bother them people. But after she lost that court case in Mississippi, and then in Washington, the Chinese were bitter and unhappy.

This story was confirmed by other old people.

An elderly man remembered the Gong Lum U.S. Supreme Court case and the intervention of the Chinese ambassador on behalf of the Chinese during the hearing of that case:

Chun Lan Ping, the Chinese Ambassador from China came to the U.S. Supreme Court hearing and asked why the Chinese were not allowed in white schools in Mississippi. You see, at that time Chinese citizens were entitled to live here and go to school here. They were protected under the Burlingame Treaty. But you see, the Supreme Court said that Gong Lum's children were not Chinese citizens. They were American citizens because they were born in the U.S. We lost the case. We might have won it if the children were Chinese nationals.

Old people recalled that between the years 1925–1935 (when the Chinese Baptist Mission School was established in Cleveland), Delta Chinese children who wanted to attend white schools had two choices: either go across the Mississippi River to Arkansas or move into the homes of other Chinese in places where school segregation laws against Chinese were not enforced. They could have private tutors. A few children attended black schools.[13] One old man recalled a private tutor.

[13]Little was said about the children who attended black schools. One wonders in what ways their attitudes may have differed from those of other Chinese children. How many attended black schools? Were any of these students eventually absorbed into the black community?

We never went to no white school. They didn't let us do it. We hired a white tutor. Daddy would hire someone to teach us. He didn't care how much it would cost him. He would hire someone as much qualified as he could. That was the best you could do then. We had several teachers who tried to teach us at the house. We'd be smarter than most of them, so we just put up with it— that's all we could get at that time. I remember one lady who almost ate us out of house and home trying to teach us English. We got rid of her the next year. She didn't know anything but how to eat.

The elderly noted that in 1936 the Delta Chinese built the Chinese Mission School with funds solicited from local businessmen and Chinese merchants in communities in Chicago, New York, and San Francisco. The Chinese purchased ten acres of land near the outskirts of town away from black and white residential neighborhoods. With help from the Baptist Home Mission Board, they built a cement-block two-story building to house out-of-town Chinese boarding students. The county hired two white schoolteachers, and the Chinese community hired one Chinese teacher from California. One old Chinese woman remembered the school.

Chinese students from the Delta boarded there and learned English from two Caucasian teachers. On top of that the Chinese pooled their money and hired a Chinese teacher from California somewhere to come and teach them Chinese, too. The English teachers were provided by the state, and you had to have twenty students for every one teacher. I don't think the children learned too much, but that was all we could do because we couldn't go to the *Bok Guey* [white] schools then. Those of us who knew a little English tried to teach our children as well as ourselves. It was hard in them days. But you see, the *Bok Guey* by paying for two teachers was willing to help us.

A segregated school system existed in Greenville prior to 1940. The Chinese had a separate school, a "shotgun shack," with twenty students from grades one through twelve. Whites had to provide a teacher for each grade level, at a cost of approximately $10,000 per year. The Chinese saw that a segregated school system was costly and suggested to the school board that five Chinese students be placed on a trial basis in the white school on the condition that if anyone objected, they would be quietly withdrawn. Only one white parent objected.

CHINESE SCHOOL OF MISSISSIPPI The Chinese School was built in 1936 by funds solicited from local businessmen and Chinese merchants from outside the Delta. Segregation laws prohibited Chinese from attending white schools and they did not want to attend black schools.

Standing from left to right are Louis Joe, Mr. Lee (Chinese teacher), and Joe Ting. Bolivar County helped the Chinese by supplying two white school teachers, and the Chinese community hired a Chinese teacher from California to teach students from grades 1–12.
Courtesy of the Joe Ting Collection

48

GREENVILLE CHINESE MISSION The Greenville Chinese Mission was organized under the auspices of the First Baptist Church of Greenville in 1934 by John Davis (church superintendent) [top row, right], Reverend William Murray [second row standing on right], and the Chinese community to teach Christianity and English to the Chinese.
Courtesy of the Joe Ting Collection

He finally approved when the Chinese pointed out to him the cost that would be incurred in maintaing a separate school system for the Chinese. Four Chinese men testified to the "purity" of the Chinese children who were allowed admission to the white school. They stipulated that "if there was one drop of black blood in a Chinese student, he was excluded."[14] Dr. Young and Mr. Alfred Mitchell, a state representative, are fondly remembered for helping the Chinese integrate a white school. The test case proved successful, and the five Chinese students graduated in the top ten of their high school class. Whites thereafter allowed the Chinese to remain in this public school.

During the Second World War white schools still remained off limits to most Chinese. An old woman described the situation:

Back in World War II I asked the white school board to let my children go to school because all of the menfolks was drafted and

[14]This expression referrred to "if you are not pure white you are black" idea prevalent among Mississippi whites at the time.

gas was rationed. They wouldn't let my children go to their school. I didn't live in Cleveland at that time, so I had to drive down to the Mission School everyday. It was so much trouble for us, and I had to run the store, too. We were law-abiding people, so we didn't fight them. I just couldn't understand it. The *Bok Guey* [whites] would take our money to build a church or something, but they wouldn't let us go to their schools. It was unfair, that's all. But we had to hold back our bitterness. Even Madame Chiang Kai-shek came to speak to the Mississippi legislature, asking them to allow the Chinese into white schools but it didn't help. After the war, things changed for the Chinese and everyone. The government tore down some of the discrimination, and the Chinese became more accepted in the Delta and could go to white schools after 1950.

Though the Chinese suffered discrimination in the quest for white social and political acceptance during the war years, they contributed to the war effort against the Japanese. They considered themselves partners with the United States in the war, especially after the repeal of the Chinese Exclusion Act in 1943.[15] Mr. Ong Beng explained how Chinese merchants contributed to the war effort:

During World War II, I was secretary-treasurer of the Chinese Against the Japanese Invasion. We raised about $50,000 for a war bond. That was a lot of money in those days. We went all over the Delta to Memphis and Arkansas to get money. Most merchants cooperated and gave a contribution. But those that didn't, we just told the milkman or wholesalers to pass the word that he didn't contribute. Sooner or later we received a contribution 'cause the merchant didn't want the wholesaler to stop him.

The first generation Chinese quickly learned that the whites wielded the power and made the law. As accommodating and law-abiding people, they "had to take what was given and make the best of it." Most respected the whites who befriended them over the years. On the other hand, they derogated those whites who refused to help them with their problems. Most of the elderly think that relationships with the whites have improved over the years and that the Chinese have finally gained the respect of this "superior group."

[15]One should keep in mind that the Chinese and the Japanese have historically been enemies.

The *Bok Guey* [whites], we all know, are in the driver's seat, and we don't give them any trouble. They respect us and we respect them. We call them Mr., Sir, and they call me P. W., and my wife, Mrs. Wong. They call me by my first name, Paul, sometimes, but that don't bother me none. Just as long as they think enough of me to come in my store and shop. You know, the *Bok Guey* don't rate themselves in the same class as us, so we got to lower ourselves sometimes. Just like in any other race there are good ones and bad ones. There are some *Bok Guey* that have done a lot for the Chinese and we invite them to our community suppers and such. They're long-time friend of the Chinese people. All of the *Bok Guey* treat us as a different kind of people than the *Lo Mok* [blacks]. They accept us as *Hon Yen* [Chinese].

Old people castigated the whites who accorded them little respect or considered them colored. They call these whites uneducated, lower-class rednecks. They probably realize, however, that the origin of the prejudice and discrimination directed against them emanated largely from the white upper class, in the form of institutionalized racial discrimination, for example, in schools and real estate. Old people stated, however, that even the rednecks treat them better today than they did before World War II.

Apparently it is easy for this generation to reconstruct the interracial situation in a favorable way for the white power structure. The civil rights legislation augmented by blacks has helped them, too. Moreover, it is always easier and safer for a minority group in any society to find some other lower-class membership responsible for its assimilation problems than to place the blame on an upper-class membership. This Chinese group, like other minority groups, admires and caters to the dominant group. Old people accept a great part of the dominant white group's political, economic, and ethnic ideology.

One old woman summarized old people's attitudes toward rednecks who gave the Chinese trouble and simultaneously revealed Chinese subordination to and admiration for the white power structure:

The *Hon Geng* [rednecks] are now not as bad as before. They used to *ha na Hon Yen* [pester the Chinese]. They were ignorant then, didn't know no better, didn't know how to treat nobody right. . . . Those *Hon Geng* used to be mean. They get out there in the fields and work all year for the big boss. Those other guys, you know, their bosses, don't treat them right, don't give them all the money's that due them. By golly, the *Hon Geng* go home and get his shotgun, come back, and hunt him up. I'll tell you the truth. My mother had a store in the Delta. She was about forty years old when she came. One day she was crying. There was two men who were *mo yung* [no good, "low down"]. Back then they had kegs of apple cider, and you drank this hot pepper vinegar which made you drunk. Those *Bok Guey doy* [white boys] would lay on the floor and open up that keg and drink until they can't move. Mama was scared to death. When they passed out, she and my father would pick each of them up by the arms and legs and throw them out the door, close it, and hope to God they wouldn't come back in the door. Now, only a redneck would do something like that. But that's the past. Now they got more education, and that makes a difference. There are still some bad ones, but there are more good ones. The Chinese are the most respected race in the South. This one *Bok Guey moo* [white lady] once said to me: "Mrs. Wong, your children just demands respect." They do, and so far we have no trouble. The *Bok Guey* [whites] are good folks.

The elderly described blacks as human beings who deserved more respect than they received. They stated that blacks had had to work themselves up from the bottom as the Chinese had done in order to improve their position. The elderly perhaps do not realize that the Chinese recipe for black upward mobility and social acceptance is questionable because of the racial factor. An excerpt from my interview with one old woman exemplifies old people's perspective on blacks.

Lots of times we loved to be more respectful to the *Hok Guey* [blacks] and everything, but it took many years to get where we are. Like, a *Hok Guey* wants you call them Mr. and Mrs., which you should call them. But if you want to keep your position with the *Bok Guey* [whites] where you have gained and accomplished, you don't let yourself get into that situation. You try to stay where you are. Now, with some *Hok Guey* [blacks], they demands respect. There is a schoolteacher who comes in once in a while and I call him Mr. Brown. Nowadays with this school integration business, you have to have a certain percentage of *Hok Guey* [black] teachers and students. Also in the factories. In about ten more years there will be *Hok Guey* mayors and high-ups all over. There's gonna be Mr. and Mrs. everywhere. They have to work themselves up, like I say. We Chinese have taken so many years down below to get up where we are now. The *Hok Guey* [blacks] will have to do the same.

I talked to many of the blacks who were ever present in and outside the Chinese grocery stores about a whole range of subjects. They felt comfortable talking to me in their own neighborhoods. Moreover, I was neither a white Southerner nor a product of the Delta Chinese community. They said the Chinese were clever, reserved merchants who made profits from high-priced groceries. Blacks are aware that the Chinese invest money in real property such as commercial buildings and houses in the black community, from which they are thought to receive large returns. On the other hand, blacks acknowledge that the Chinese merchants donate to black churches and athletic clubs. Generally blacks voice ambivalent attitudes toward the Chinese; they say the Chinese are money-grubbing exploiters but also decent, hard-working, charitable, clever businessmen who provide a service to the black community. Blacks accept without rancor the fact that the Chinese do not mix with them socially on an intimate basis. In short, blacks acknowledge and accept the triracial society.

One Saturday afternoon I encountered a group of three blacks approximately twenty-five years old sipping beer as they stood on the sidewalk next to a Chinese grocery store. They gave me their views of the Mississippi Chinese.

Larry, the most verbal of the three blacks, spoke first. "The Chinese, the way I see it, mind their own business, take care of their families, and are very friendly people. We call each other by our first names. The Chinese are real nosey and clever businessmen. They want to know everything about you, but they don't tell you anything about themselves. They definitely like money, and their prices are sky high—and that's real low down, if you know what I mean."

"What do they do for the black people?" I asked.

"Oh, they sometimes give money to the black church and the athletic club."

"How do the customers feel about the high prices?"

"You know that as independent grocers they can juggle their prices like they want to. They want to make money, it's that, pure and simple. And they make it off the black folk who are their number one customers. I know they own a lot of property, land, and buildings in the black and white community. They play the white man's game better than white people do."

Sammy, one of the group members, added a comment at this point. "Yeah, the Chinese stick together, but they argue with each other. The old man is all right, he's a real easygoing man. But his wife's a bitch. She's always raising hell around the store and arguing with other Chinese down the street."

"What do they argue about?"

"Money! They love money. And children. Their children tell me they're sick and tired of the old man and old lady trying to run their lives. In fact, one of his daughters just married a white man and had to move away. You know they're not happy about that one bit."

The elderly blacks I talked to took a friendlier, more charitable view of the Chinese. (Older blacks are also friendlier to whites than are younger blacks.) For example, one man about sixty years old made this comment about his generation's views toward Chinese merchants:

> The Chinese and his family and kin have all been here for a long, long time. We've all traded with these stores down the street since I can remember. The Chinese sold us everything we needed. Like when my wife had her first baby, the woman [midwife] who helped her have it sent me down to Jack's to pick up towels, aspirin, and things like that. I didn't have much money then, but Jack said I could pay him back later. We would pay up when we could, and they were friendly about it, too. We all get along here real good. The Chinese are good people.

The whites I talked to about the Chinese expressed highly favorable attitudes toward them. Whites view them as an acceptable people within the Delta, clever, middle-class merchants who work hard to make a decent living. Whites report that Chinese children are very intelligent and competitive in school and that Chinese adults are good citizens and good Christians. One white businessman's sketch is representative of the attitude of most Delta whites.

> The Chinese here are good Christian people and always seem to follow the laws. They are hard-working, smart people who are wealthy. Their children are bright and intelligent and very inde-

54

pendent. Most of them no longer follow the old people's ways. They are middle class and get along with both blacks and whites. My son goes to school with them, and they're always winning some kind of award. The Mississippi Chinese are a proud people and have made a lot of progress in the Delta. Everyone respects them a whole lot now.

Old people see themselves primarily as first-generation Delta Chinese or Chinese but never refer to themselves as Chinese Americans. In fact they report very tenuous ties to Chinese or Chinese communities outside Mississippi, that is, with a few of their children and grandchildren. Many told me the Chinese people on the West Coast and those from New York and Chicago were strange people quite different from themselves. They also define themselves as Christians, patriarchs, successful grocery store men, property owners, counselors to the young, teachers and bridges to the past, good family providers, leaders in the church and the Chinese community. They know they are at the top of the deference hierarchy in the Delta Chinese community and exhibit exceptional pride in having founded this community. All members of this group describe themselves as following the traditional Chinese way of thinking and acting. They also voice pride and happiness in United States citizenship. Old people wish to preserve much of their "Chineseness" within a Mississippi Delta context. They reluctantly accept the Americanization process in the lives of the young. In short, they prefer a pluralistic America where they can remain Delta Chinese. Significantly, they do not seem to realize that the loss of Chinese religion and language makes such an identity untenable for future generations.

Old people view the world as a place to maintain a Delta Chinese existence for themselves and their families. Their world is a small, well-ordered, provincial, isolated, closed society far removed from larger Chinese enclaves. Their perspectives, ideas, and activities are concrete rather than intellectual and center on the family, work, the Chinese community, and the church. Old people's primary mission is the perpetuation of what they call "the Chinese way." They underscore the significance of the family as the main institution for transmitting the Chinese world view to the younger generation. These elders know that the overseas Chinese have solved social and economic problems through their history by maintaining a Chinese cultural perspective. The Mississippi Chinese have committed themselves to this task in the Delta. Old people, however, do not seem to understand that it is easier for the overseas Chinese in Asian third-world countries near mainland China to perpetuate a Chinese world view than it is for the Delta Chinese who are far removed from mainland China in space, time, and culture.

One old woman told me:

> The Chinese go everywhere to foreign lands to make a better living. There are some even in New Guinea. They live in the jungle. But we came to the Delta to stay, to live, and raise our families here. We are different from the *Bok Guey* [whites] and we are different from the *Hok Guey* [blacks]; we are Chinese. We didn't work for ourselves all these years. We worked to give our children the best we could so they could go to college. And all of us have done that. The Chinese family is strong—when someone succeed, we all succeed. Now it is up to the younger generation to follow in our footsteps and carry on the Chinese ways.

Old people perceive their world, the Delta, as a microcosm of the wider capitalist world. This world to them consists of thousands of competitive arenas where the hard-working, virtuous, and thrifty compete, endure, and prosper, while the lazy, wanton, and incompetent fail and "go under." They claim that the Chinese succeed everywhere because they lead simple lifestyles, are free from vices, and work hard. The Chinese philosophy prescribes a simple life with attention to maintaining health, saving money, avoiding conflicts, and giving and taking in moderation. One old woman expressed this view.

> I don't spend my life on drinking and smoking and none of my friends do, either. Old people have learned that the only way to get ahead in this world is to live a simple healthy life, save money, and don't bother no one. Those who run like the hare tire themselves out quickly. But those who stay where they are and build on what they have will endure. I made and spent much of my money on my children. Now they are all grown up and successful. . . . that is my happiness. I have taught them well. I tell them that the world is rough out there. They have to get in there and compete with all the others. They must not be greedy and brittle. They must be like bamboo, which bends in the storm yet grows

high toward the skies. So my children have been taught to give
and take. . . . that is the way of nature . . . and life. You give a little
and take a little. Always leave some for someone else. You have
seen many Chinese grocery stores on this street and many families, but there is still enough room so that everyone can make a
good living and be happy.

The elderly place a premium on education, in keeping with
the Chinese traditional practice of rewarding scholarship with
social advancement. One old man outlined the way to success
and bragged about his people:

> If you were to ask what it takes to survive and be respected in this
> world—I will tell you. Money and education. The Chinese started
> at the bottom with no money, no education. That's why they
> didn't get any respect. but we have worked hard to give these
> things to our children. Chinese are now prosperous and respected
> in Mississippi. They have money, brains, and education. They are
> now at the top!

I heard only success stories during this investigation. Certainly there are those who failed, but I did not learn of their
lives. Success stories are anchored in belief systems far removed
from the traditional Chinese ideology in space and time. Old
people, in short, are more Americanized then they realize. This,
of course, has been the rule for many other American minority
groups. The insistence on the "Chinese way" reflects a traditional Chinese upbringing. A major component of this Chinese
way in the Delta appears to be an emphasis on form rather than
content, that is, attention to etiquette and proper conduct at all
times rather than to any specific Chinese behavior. The preoc-
cupation with courtesy fits in nicely with the Southern pattern
of correctness; one always acts like a gentleman or lady regardless of the situation and regardless of how one really feels.

Old People's View of Other Community Groups
Businessmen

Businessmen are the sons, relatives, and friends of the first
generation. Old people describe some of them as more successful than others. Most "had done all right." Those who were
frugal, industrious, family oriented, and committed to the Chi-

nese ways of thinking, living, and operating a business became successful. Those who failed to follow these tenets "had to leave the Delta for somewhere else to make a living." I was not told who failed, where they went, or what later became of them. Mr. Soon Lee gave the following recipe for success:

> In this *san yee* [business] you've got to know what you're doing. You have to *nam thleng* [think things out] before you make a move. You know, figure out how much this proposition costs, how much money you get out of it. In other words, you have to have some guts and take some risks. Those that are nice guys don't make the money. They give all of their stock away to friends or let people steal it. To stay ahead you got to save money, work hard, discipline the children, and teach them the family business and the Chinese way. You see, everyone's got to help out.

Elders identify successful businessmen on the basis of the location of enterprise, economic prosperity, and future business plans. One elderly merchant compared those who "do well" with those who "just stay above the water."

> There are some businessmen who have made a success in the Chinese community. They followed the Chinese ways, saved their money, and invested it wisely. Now a few young businessmen own large supermarkets in the best section of town and do a large business. But at first they had to do like we did . . ., make it in a small store in *Hok Guey Fao* [black community]. These people have made a good living. Most of them own nice homes, too. Then you have those businessmen who are in a bad location or maybe a bad neighborhood. They can't get anywhere now and never will. All they can do is try to stay above the water. Their stores don't make much money because the *Lo Mok* [blacks] can go other places to shop. But most of them still do O.K., and some still make good money like I did. Then there are a few restaurant owners. These people got a new idea and they can make plenty of money. What else is a Chinese going to do? Old Chinese can't read and write English very good. It's too late to go to school. He can't compete against the chain stores any more. . . . so there you have it. 'Course I don't have a business in the white part of town. The young businessmen can afford to take a chance and move out. Either you make money in this world or you don't. For myself, I would rather have the cash, and you know, I have done pretty good in the grocery business.

Old people place businessmen second in the Chinese community's deference hierarchy. Because of economic status, age and occupational similarity to first-generation members businessmen enjoy a closer affinity with old people than do other Chinese community groups; the similarities extend to the way they look at life, the Chinese way, language, diet, art, child-rearing practices, family leadership, respect for elders, and business practices. The elderly noted that businessmen confronted economic and family problems unheard of in "the early days." For example, today's merchants, unlike their predecessors, face competition from chain and convenience stores throughout the Delta. The old people also mentioned that the second generation's children and wives are less dutiful. This condition was attributed to the influence of modern life. Old people say that businessmen today are also different from themselves in being more Americanized and better educated, possessing more language skills, being more mobile, and having more time to relax and enjoy life. They regret that businessmen today are more concerned with the present and the future than with the past. The elderly assume that businessmen view them as the respected, successful, experienced, and courageous group that created and perpetuated a Chinese identity and culture within the Mississippi Delta.

Professionals

Professionals (pharmacists, accountants, business managers, nurses, teachers, and so forth) are men and women who have brought honor and pride to their families and to the Mississippi Delta Chinese. The elderly are overjoyed to have children, grandchildren, relatives, and friends in the ranks of the professional class. They look forward to seeing them earn degrees so that they can announce, for example, that there is a "pharmacist in the family." Old people, self-styled traditionalists, know that professionalization is costly. One old man lamented:

We old people are afraid that when the children go to college to become engineers, teachers, doctors, and lawyers, they no longer hold onto the Chinese ways. And I can see why, because these children have to mix with the *Bok Guey* [whites] and do social things with them in order to get ahead. But soon they like the American way better than the Chinese way. They are no longer real *Hon Yen* [Chinese] but *Bok Guey]* [whites].

59

The elderly had mixed feelings about the professional rewards of education and occupational attainment. One old
woman disclosed her fears about the cost of success, the the loss
of Chinese ways, the probable loss of the professional population, and the dearth of professional openings in the Delta:

> We old people are so proud of our sons and daughters who are
> now professionals and have a good job. We see that they have a
> big future in front of them because they make lots of money and
> can give their children the best things and opportunities that we
> never had. Plus professionals have education which we did not
> have and could not give them at home. But I hope that this
> generation will not forget their Chinese heritage. They say that
> we old people are so set in our ways and thinking. . . . I have
> feared it all along that the new generation is losing all desire to
> keep the Chinese ways. They see the American way as being the
> best. School has helped them, but it has not helped them. They
> are now successful like the high-class *Lo Fan* [whites], but they
> forget so soon that they are *Hon Yen* [Chinese]. It is so sad. . . . It
> would be our wishes to keep these professionals here in Missis-
> sippi, but there are not enough jobs here, and they must go where
> the chances are better for them.

The old people criticize the professionals for speaking too
much English at home, following Western health-care practices
rather than Chinese medicine, mixing predominantly with
whites, staying away from home too long, eating American
food, and not being religious enough. They say that professionals are becoming white in orientation, that is, they have more
white than Chinese friends, and that they socialize frequently
with people on the basis of class rather than because they are
Chinese. The elderly bemoan the fact that professionals have
less in common with businessmen (their parents) than they do
with other professionals. They admire professionals, however,
for making "good money," possessing advanced degrees, lead-
ing more independent lives, and enjoying more social prestige
than businessmen in the wider community. And of course the
professionals' success is their own success. I received no reports
about would-be professionals who dropped out of school or
changed their course of study for one reason or another. Certainly all who start do not finish. Old people believe professionals view them as frugal, revered, and sage people who still think

in the traditional way and follow somewhat outmoded practices.

College Students

Old people view college students as a group who have left home to become part of another world, the secular world of higher education. They note that this group is unlike the older professionals because it is still struggling and facing a technologically advanced world, which requires a greater sacrifice of their Chinese cultural bonds. The first generation fears that college students now on the road to professional training and success will eventually merge with the American mainstream. The elders complain that college students rarely come home to visit, seldom speak Chinese, eat Chinese food infrequently, and show little interest in Chinese members of the opposite sex. Such behavior indicates to them that college students are wrapped up in their own world, a world beyond the Delta. The following observations by an old woman illustrate old people's insights regarding the breakdown of Chinese ways among college students:

> The younger generation who go to college these days see the world much different than us old people who were born and raised in China. College kids have a world of their own. When they come home during the summer they are much different than when they left. Each year in school they change, and I have seen it. They don't care about Chinese customs any more or that they are Chinese. They say to me: "Grandma, I am a person, not Chinese." I cannot believe it when they tell me that! They are still good children and very disciplined, but they no longer hold onto the Chinese ways I have taught them. They eat hamburgers instead of rice. They date the Caucasians instead of their own people ... and they also marry a few of them. They don't even like to speak Chinese any more. They speak *Fan Wah* [English language] all the time. They are a bunch of *jook sing* [the hollow part of the bamboo; lacking any Chinese substance]. Everything is changing so quickly since I came to Meigok [America]. They have strayed away further than some of the older professionals. We are afraid this will be the way with each new generation, and we can't help it.

Members of the first generation consider college students industrious and committed workers struggling to make a place in the world for themselves. They are proud of the good grades, awards, and honors that college students earn at school. They appreciate college students who still show them respect by attending occasional Chinese community activities. I received no reports of students who did not receive good grades. Certainly some must be mediocre students or academic failures. How do they feel about these students? What do these students do to please them?

The elderly think that college students fluctuate between a Chinese and a white identity. They hope that these young people will "turn out to be" as Chinese as possible. One old man said: "We did it in the Delta when we first came here; we made it for ourselves. And if we can do it, they can too, and still be Chinese." First-generation members do not take into account the fact that they, unlike the college students, were socialized in China and that the college students are third-generation, not first-generation, Americans. None talked about those who did not go to college. I pressed them on this point but received only vague answers, for example: "I don't know about any," "Guess they go to work in the grocery," "I guess they get a job some place," "Why do you keep asking me that?" Old people think college students view them as outmoded, stubborn, frugal people who are still loved and held in high esteem. They also know that some college women do not want them to interfere in their social life.

Young People

Members of the first generation defined young people as an impressionable group that can be readily taught the Chinese way. They pointed out that young people still lived with their parents and were nearby. Therefore, the old are able to enjoy the young and teach them the Chinese way. To the old the young people represent the future. The elderly explain that young people are not as confused as the professionals and the college students. One old woman at a wedding expressed her joy in knowing that young people have not lost the cherished Chinese way:

Young people make me so happy. I have seven grandchildren myself. I always look forward to Christmas and other times during the year when they come and visit me. You know children grow up so fast. before you know it they're in high school and then college. My grandchildren are very well trained because their parents see to it that they learn who they are. They come up to me and call me *Ah Yeen* [Grandmother] and it makes me happy that they can speak Chinese and know how to give old people respect. Now that the Chinese are very well respected in Mississippi and have prosperous businesses, I think the young people benefit greatly from this. They know they are Chinese and not just another *Lo Fan* [white]. Yes, young people are proud that they are Chinese. We have taught them to be that way.

In speaking with me the elderly did not acknowledge the fact that young people speak English in most situations and that their Chinese is limited. Moreover, I have seen children "show off" in front of Chinese Delta parents and grandparents as they do in other cultural groups. I do not mean that old people falsify their views about young people or that these views are incorrect. To the contrary, I agree with them, but their statements here about the younger generation appear exaggerated. One would expect this to be the case because most grandparents in all cultures embellish anecdotes about their grandchildren.

Young people are the pride and joy of their elders, who claimed that they would do well because they were secure, adjusted, and well-disciplined individuals—and better cared for physically than previous generations. The old people boast that no young people are juvenile delinquents and that they do not have boyfriends or girlfriends while in school.

It should be kept in mind that the first generation's views of and hopes for young people refer to a captive audience still living among a group of protective parents and grandparents. Young people turn into adults quickly, whether as college students, professionals, or members of society in some other capacity. It is likely that today's young people will wander further from the Chinese way than the second generation of young people, because of the inexorable process of Americanization. Moreover, the next generation of old people will be less Chinese than those of today. The romanticized (but to some extent real) Chinese way cannot be followed closely by a generation that is Christian, speaks English, and is far removed in time and space from the traditional China of their grandparents—who themselves no longer wholly follow the Chinese way. Old people believe that young people see them as friendly, venerable grandpas, grandmas, uncles, aunts, and baby-sitters who are esteemed and loved by everyone.

Women

Old women are industrious, strong-willed, good mothers to their children and eager perpetuators of Chinese culture. The elders have watched old women work next to their husbands for many years in order to provide for their children. The old people claim that these women have fulfilled their Chinese duty; that is, they have reared well-disciplined children whom they have taught to be Christians as well as Chinese. One old man expounded on the place of old women:

> The Chinese women in the Delta are hard-working people, especially the older ones. They have had to raise their children and keep the family together during the many hard times the Chinese people went through. They have had to work side by side with their husbands to make money to feed and clothe their children and to send them back to school. It was hard times back then, with the depression and the war. But the old women made it. It is the woman's job to teach the children the Chinese ways. It is her duty to discipline the children and to keep them out of trouble. The old ways have always worked, and the women should be given credit for the survival of the Chinese in *Nam Fong* [the South].

The men define their aging wives as partners in the struggle to establish and maintain the Chinese identity in the Delta and as role models for the ongoing generation. In turn, these men think that old women look upon them as honored, respected, successful Chinese leaders who carry on the Chinese way. It could be that old people tend to exaggerate their own virtuous roles when they look back over three or four decades of marriage. However, no negative views were reported.

The first generation considers young married women assertive and independent. To them this group is too westernized and follows too closely American child-rearing practices: overindulgence, loose discipline, freedom, and insufficient training in parental respect.

One elderly woman spoke to this point:

64

The young married women have become westernized by education. They also have more money to spend these days. They forget the Chinese ways and do things their way. They are spoiled, and they spoil their children, giving them anything they want. When I visit my children and see my grandchildren, they just say "hey" and rush out the door. They don't even want to sit and talk to their grandmother. I think I know why. It's because these young kids don't have to work in the store like the older generation, so they don't know what hard work is. Also, the young married couples mix with the *Bok Guey* [whites] so much that they become just like them.

Here we see a contradictory view of young people not expressed when the old people were discussing young people per se. Probably there is animosity toward some of the young married women as well as displeasure with some of the young people, those not previously eulogized, who may not be so respectful and obedient.

The elderly reported that young married women possessed a hybrid Chinese identity, one mixed with American culture and one that their elders would like to see reversed, although no one expressed ideas as to how this reversal could be accomplished. Old people probably have no answers to the problem they perceive and know that a reversal of the younger group's identity is impossible. The young married women were described as having good jobs, being married to good providers, and working hard to be good mothers in economically secure home environments. Old people stated that young married women pictured them as old-fashioned, bossy, and domineering (but helpful) grandparents.

Old people view young unmarried women as furture wives and mothers in the Chinese community. They were disconcerted by the independence of this group and grumbled that most of them had been influenced too much by a larger Caucasian world. To the first generation's way of thinking, this group displays less dignity, dependence, and virtue than previous generations. One old woman addresses the problem in this commentary:

Many of the young women who are still here in the Delta will find good Chinese boys to marry. They have remained Chinese, stayed at home, and have been good Chinese girls. Then there are some others who these days lack dignity. Some of them, you know, *san lai* [act primitive]. Some drink alcohol, and some smoke cigarettes in public. No real Chinese man would want to marry that kind of woman. Some young women even take baby pills [birth control pills] and they are not married! I can't understand that. Old people did not teach their daughters to be disrespectful. But today's society is so different . . ., full of hippies. A Chinese woman must save her dignity, look and act like a lady, be proud to be a woman—not man. This is the way she must follow if she is to attract a decent man. But some of the young ones have taken another path. Thank God many are still good Chinese girls and wear bras and save themselves for marriage.

Elders confide that these modernized females follow too closely the American way in dating, leisure activities, mode of dress, topics of conversation, and general attitude and demeanor. Many are criticized for acting as independent as men and have forgotten that men and women must play different roles. Some claim that a few young unmarried women date Caucasians and that many seem to be more interested in pursuing a career than in finding a good Chinese man for marriage. To old people, a young woman's central goal should be marriage, not a career. Some young women are regarded as even more Americanized than Chinese males of their age. The elderly people fear that rapid assimilation endangers the young Chinese male's masculinity as well as the female's feminity. I will discuss this question further in chapter 6.

The elderly report that young unmarried women have a contradictory attitude toward them: they respect and love them but at the same time consider them to be old-fashioned, prying, suspicious critics who are eager to push them into a traditional marriage. The conflict between these two groups is predictable, but it is likely to be reduced in future generations because future old people will have been socialized in the United States rather than in China.

I conclude this chapter on old people with a group of excerpts from statements on various subjects that seem to me to illustrate better than my narrative could how the first generation views its experiences and relationship to succeeding generations.

On caring for children:

Whenever my children leave their kids with me, I enjoy cooking them rice and Chinese food instead of the meat loaf they get at home. I speak to them in Chinese and teach them how to say the numbers. Sometimes I will teach them a Chinese song, one that I learned as a little child in China.

On helping young people start out in business:

I helped my children get started in the drug store business. That business is just like the grocery business except drugs are marked up higher than beans—and you get rich pretty quick. These kids got an education, but they still consult with me before they make the big decisions. This shows respect for my knowledge, and it helps them out, too.

On choosing a mate:

The old women are more worried about their children than I am. But I will tell you this: I know of many Chinese and Caucasian marriages, and they soon fall apart. My son told me a long time ago that he wanted to marry this certain *Bok Guey nu* [Caucasian girl], and I told him if you do that, then everything we have taught you, all that we have given you, will all go down the drain. I told him to think about it, and he did. He changed his mind and married a Chinese girl. I think that was the best way. He now respects us for our advice.

On settling a family dispute:

My daughter and her mother-in-law, a traditional Chinese woman, have had arguments over the past two years since my daughter married. They all live under one roof and they fight because the young one wants to do things her way and the old woman thinks she can boss both her son and my daughter. That is the old Chinese way—the young must yield to the old, but I don't think it is the right way. Everyone should work together in harmony. My daughter could no longer stand it and called me for help. I went to their home one day and told my daughter it was dishonorable to treat her mother-in-law, an old woman, with such disrespect. But I also told the old woman that her petty and selfish ways could not be tolerated any longer. I proposed that each of them learn to live with one another without all this *ow geng* [arguing, bitterness] or else my husband would be called in to stop it—and his words are feared. The two women mended their ways quickly and saved face. All three parties became reconciled.

The Businessmen

Businessmen occupy the second position in the Mississippi Chinese community's deference hierarchy. The majority of these property owners, the sons, relatives, and friends of first-generation members, range in age from the mid-thirties to the late fifties. Businessmen see themselves as educated, successful owner-operators of grocery stores, self-service markets, liquor stores, and restaurants in the Mississippi Delta. Though a few started their own businesses, most inherited capital or property from their fathers. Some have accumulated enough money to invest in new business ventures involving real estate, farms, gift shops, art supplies, electronics shops, and occasionally the stockmarket. Wives and children help in the family business and are considered assets to social and economic success.

Businessmen told me they were taught the traditional Chinese ways by their parents, the old people. All speak English and Cantonese. Most had learned English in either the Delta or the Chinese Mission School. Some few had studied under a hired tutor at home. They learned the Delta vernacular from black and white customers in Chinese grocery stores and Cantonese in the family situation as they communicated with parents, especially the mother. Businessmen, U.S. citizens by birth, were drafted and spent time in the U.S. military services. Some later joined the American Legion or the Veterans of Foreign Wars. Service-related activities have further accustomed them to the American way. Most are not members of community service organizations such as the Jaycees, Chamber of Commerce, or the Lions Club.[1] The majority attend various churches throughout the Delta: Baptist, Methodist, Presbyterian, Catholic, and the Chinese Baptist Church and its missions. The vast majority are Baptist and members of Chinese Baptist churches.

Businessmen claim to have stable, happy marriages with Chinese-American wives. Divorce is rare. Most of these people have families with five or six children and live in modest, unpretentious homes built in the 1950s in lower-middle-class white residential areas. Some of the more prosperous occupy houses in new white upper-middle-class neighborhoods near other Chinese homes of similar value, dwellings that range in value from $40,000 to $100,000 each. They declared a preference for privately made business investments rather than for any conspicuous display of wealth, and I observed that their life-style bore out the claim.

Businessmen wear plain clothes in the everyday round of life and stylish conservative suits on Sunday and at festive Chinese community functions. Few own Cadillacs, but most drive expensive, late-model Buicks, their most obvious status symbol. Their wives generally dress conservatively and on special occasions (Sundays, weddings, holidays) wear diamond, gold, and jade jewelry. Many of these expensive pieces are heirlooms.

This second-generation group told me they were middle class, though most owned property (apart from their homes) worth anywhere from $80,000 to $190,000. Businessmen avow that their class awareness is based on community respectability as well as property. However, they understand very clearly that respectability and wealth are not separable and that without wealth respectability is tenuous. Businessmen refer to lower-class people as uneducated, manipulable primitives. Anyone can succeed if he works hard enough, according to them. They define and look upon the lower-class "redneck" whites much as

[1]No reasons were reported for this tendency. Membership in such organizations will probably increase as Chinese engage more frequently in business outside black neighborhoods. There is some evidence now to indicate such a trend.

do their middle-class white counterparts.[2] Businessmen sense their vulnerability as a third racial group in the Delta and speak of the necessity to work hard for survival in a triethnic community. They stress the imperatives of getting along with blacks and whites, accumulating property, and preserving their dignity as Delta Chinese. All claim that their parents gave them a Chinese identity, but all are proud of being U.S. citizens and respectable members of the Mississippi Delta community.

Businessmen at Home

Businessmen view themselves at home as successful, respected family providers. They claim an internalized Confucian family tradition. For example, they were taught as children to subordinate individual interests to the welfare of the family. Businessmen see themselves as patriarchs and disciplinarians. They teach their children the Chinese way, that is, obedience, filial piety, respect for the elderly, parents, and relatives, a Delta Chinese identity, thrift, industry, and endogamy. They also try to supervise their children's courtship and mate selections. Wives help in socializing and controlling the young. They play a complementary and more lenient role than their husbands.[3] Businessmen share an affinity with old people in the areas of child-rearing practices, sex roles, familial orientation, Chinese customs, art and language, and respect for elders. The main goal is to make money to provide children with a college education and a comfortable style of living. They place high priority on the values of initiative and education, exemplified by such adages as: "The money is out there, you just have to go out and get it" and "You can lose everything but a good educa-

[2]See Julian B. Roebuck and Ronald L. Neff, "The Multiple Reality of the Redneck: Toward a Grounded Theory of the Southern Class Structure, *Studies in Symbolic Interaction,* vol. 31 Chicago: JAI Press, 1981), pp. 233–262.

[3]Traditionally, social control was exercised from within the Chinese community. Disputes have always been handled and settled by Chinese elders and businessmen. These individuals said that help is never needed from outsiders. Serious and flagrant violations of unacceptable behavior call for action by the families involved. If no such action is taken, leaders in the Chinese community intervene and arbitrate the matter. I probed in this area but received no examples.

tion." They seldom express overt affection in public for their wives or children.

Sons and daughters are asked to revere and obey parents and older family members. Devotion to the family is expected at all times. Children are required to adhere to the declarations passed down by fathers and mothers. Businessmen consider disrespectful and disgraceful conduct a breach of their authority, action which dishonors the family and causes the individual as well as the family unit to lose face. Disobedience, in short, diminishes family solidarity. All family members are expected to protect the family name at all times.

Businessmen explain that their children and other Delta Chinese of all groups who persist in serious misbehavior are isolated from the family and the Chinese community. They did not report any specific instances, however. I probed one influential merchant, who gave me the following account: "You see, we had a few common-law marriages back between 1910 and 1930. You know, between Chinese men and black women. You know what we did. We didn't have anything to do with them, that's all. We didn't try to break up their marriages. We just didn't invite them to our houses or parties. At that time the Chinese men couldn't bring his wife over, so some of them needed companionship. Some fell in love. . . ."

Businessmen realize that filial piety can only operate in a traditional family environment where property, patriarchy, and a clearly defined division of labor obtain and that present-day Chinese families are moving toward a more equalitarian American family system. Most businessmen I talked to claimed they would allow their children to date middle-class whites, something they said their fathers would never have accepted on grounds of endogamy. Most concede they would reluctantly accept Chinese-white marriages but never marriages with blacks. The businessmen may be defensive in their disapproval of Chinese-white marriages. That is, they might disapprove of Chinese-white marriages less if the Delta whites and the Chinese community were more accepting of such liaisons.

Businessmen care for their elderly parents and relatives in times of need. For example, one businessman recalled the death of his sister's husband, who owned a store: "When the old man died, I went over to help her with the store by stacking groceries and such so that she could take care of other things that needed to be done. I didn't have to, I just felt it was my duty to help out." Businessmen take care of their feeble parents at home instead of "sending them to rest homes like the whites do." One merchant commented: "When the *Lo Fan* [whites] send their mothers and fathers to old people's homes, we don't understand that. We try to care for them at home, that's where they are mostly happy. Even the *Lo Mok* [blacks] know this and respect the old. It is much better that way. They are part of the family too."

Businessmen's homes are comfortable but modest. Furnishings do not reflect an ostentatious display of wealth. Much of the furniture and household appliances are from the earlier days when the family was not so well-to-do. A few Chinese art objects are evident, such as Chinese porcelain vases and figurines, ivory sculptures of animals and sages, hand-painted china, silk embroidered wildlife scenes framed under glass, and picture scrolls hand painted on bamboo. These, along with chilren's graduation pictures, are found in living rooms. Art pieces are acquired as inheritances and as marriage or other gifts from friends and relatives. The owners claim that these objects act as symbols of a Chinese identity for themselves and their children.

Businessmen usually come home around 9:30 P.M. after closing their stores. They seldom change clothes but remove their shoes and don a pair of Chinese slippers, sit in a favorite chair, read the newspaper, watch television, talk to children, and wait for the wives to cook a Chinese supper. One evening after work Mr. Toy Gee spoke to me about the welfare system, investments, fathers, and sons.

"They ought to do away with the welfare system," said Mr. Toy Gee. "When the government cuts down on welfare, that means people can't buy much groceries from me, and I have to extend more credit. I don't like to tie up my money. I like to invest it." Of his real estate investments in the black community where he owns a grocery store, he said, "They don't pay but sixty dollars a month and sometimes it ain't worth it to collect the rent on the houses or to have to fix a window that's busted out."[4]

Mr. Toy Gee recalled his father's patriarchal authority in the home. "My father was a strong-willed man. When he spoke, everyone listened. That was the way back then. I remember him talking to my sister's husband before she married him. He really scared the guy—told him that if he married his daughter, he'd have to make lots of money or he'd be in big trouble. . . . It almost scared him away. And you know, that's how all of us were raised, to honor and respect our parents, but especially our father. . . . I mean he was a *hao chuey* . . ., a big boss!" Mr. Toy Gee told how he fostered Chinese filial piety in his children. "All of my children were brought up to honor their parents. They are hard-working, intelligent, and honest children. They respect us. We love them, but we show our love in a different way, different from the *Bok Guey* [whites]. We show care and concern and keep our dignity with the children. I know sometimes it's hard for them to understand it because they have learned the American ways, and they think we are too strict and reserved. But that's the Chinese way to teach their children discipline, respect, and honor."

Businessmen stress education and hard work to their children. One merchant took a hard line:

> I tell my children that if they are ever going to make a success here or anywhere else, they have to study hard. I tell them that the outside world is very different from the inside world at home. It is here at home that they must prepare themselves to face the problems of a hard, cold world out there. The money is out there to be made, but they have to learn how to get it and keep it. When the children come home from school every day, they work in the store. They do their homework in there. I don't let them play sports after school like the *Bok Guey* [whites] let their kids. I'm a little strict on them, but I got to be. Other Chinese families do the same thing. That's the only way to get ahead. You got to give up playing right now. It's now work, hard work, but they can play

[4]Note the inconsistent reasoning here. Without the welfare system he probably would not be in business. If he were not making money on rental property, he would not rent. He is talking good old American business double-talk. He wants it both ways—always.

later after they graduate or when they get older. There will be plenty of time then.

Businessmen informed me that decisions concerning mate selection were strongly influenced by parents. The mother and father usually dictate who the children are to date and, therefore, who they marry. Children manage to choose the individual mate, but the mother and father dictate the type. The children chose individuals of the type that met with parental consent. Businessmen claimed that several factors operate in marital choice: family approval, family background, being Chinese, money, property, and education. Therefore, according to businessmen, mate selection is based not on "romantic love" but on more mundane criteria. Marriages, they say, are no longer iron-clad arrangements but still join two families as well as the bride and groom.

Businessmen prefer endogamy and often counsel their children to make friends with those eligible for marriage. Sometimes relatives are called in to help find a suitable mate. One businessman explained:

> Several of my girls are already married. They married fine young men who have steady jobs and can go somewhere. Now I have one more daughter to *ga huey* [marry off]. Her mother and I emphasized school while she was in college, and she was tops in her class. But now that she's been out of school for two years, we are worried that she might not find someone to marry. We have tried to talk her into going out with some of the young Chinese boys, but she's very particular. My sister-in-law even tried to introduce her to a young man and she turned him down. There really aren't many Chinese boys to be friends with around here in the Delta. The pickings are slim. Maybe she will find someone to marry somewhere else. But one thing is for sure, he's got to be Chinese. We all feel the Chinese should stick with Chinese. Interracial marriages don't make and never did.[5]

Though businessmen attempt to enforce endogamy among their children, violations do occur. One merchant's reactions

[5]Because businessmen exhibit a more modern attitude toward Chinese-White marriages than do old people and realize the inadequacy of potential Chinese mates for their children in the Delta, they are ambivalent about mixed marriages. However, they feel strongly against marriage to lower-class whites and especially marriage to any blacks.

are probably typical: "I'm not against it [mixed marriages], but I don't like it. It just brings problems. Just like the hen and the duck, when the Caucasian boy comes to a Chinese girl's house he feels out of place. You cannot be just happy in your house. You have to go outside, you know, with the society. But if they just go and do it, then I have to accept it."

Businessmen at Work

Businessmen see themselves at work as a group of successful proprietors in a triethnic community. Some have reinvested their profits from the grocery business in other small businesses such as gift shops, electronics shops, and art supply stores, which are frequently run by family members. They say these new enterprises are capital investments to meet the changing economy of the Delta. One merchant described his business acumen when profits in the grocery store business declined:

> I operated a store for about ten years, but decided I had to either go into wholesaling or do something else to compete in these times. So I went into the restaurant business, a Chinese restaurant. Now when I first started, the *Bok Guey* [whites] were not used to eating Chinese food, but over the years they developed a taste for it. Plus my restaurant is nicely decorated for businessmen to bring their friends and family to dine. I have a nice bar and lounge and the atmosphere suits their taste. I see that this business is really going good. I serve good food and teach my waitresses to treat the customers right. Most Chinese don't eat here too often. Maybe for a party or something because they know the price of food and can eat at home. You got to invest wisely, or you don't make money. You see, things have changed in the Delta and you got to change with it. Like Mr. Eng Hok across town, who owns a stereo electronic store. His father put him in business. Boy, he makes good business and lots of money, but he went to college, see. I didn't. All I had was good luck going for me.[6]

[6]The interiors of Chinese restaurants in the Delta were decorated in an oriental motif. On the dining room walls hung framed wildlife scenes embroidered on silk. Room dividers were made from teak and black lacquered screens with simulated inlaid jade. Chinese lanterns contributed to the exotic atmosphere. A quick glance at the spacious dining room, banquet room, and bar indicated an upper-class milieu, as did the prices on the menu, and the customers appeared affluent.

The businessmen who had followed in the old people's footsteps as small independent grocery merchants confided that their economic position was tenuous. They receive intense competition from large chain supermarkets and small convenience stores. Nevertheless, they insist that their small stores are still making money. Businessmen claim to perform a necessary economic function for long-standing black customers in the neighborhood who still buy on credit. They point out that knowing how to give credit places them at an advantage over whites, who as a rule do not extend credit. I visited Mr. Tong Mein at his store one day when he described the economic competition with whites (especially the recently built white-owned convenience store down the street from his business), his knowledge of how to extend credit to blacks, competition from chain supermarkets, his symbiotic relationship with long-time customers, and the advantages of large supermarkets.

It was two o'clock in the afternoon and business was slow in his store, which was located on a main street bordering the black neighborhood. I asked, "Do you think that the new *Bok Guey* [white] convenience store is pulling in much business these days?"

Mr. Tong Mein thought for a few seconds. "Well, right now not as good as when he first opened up a year ago. He had a lot of business then, and some of my *Hok Guey* [black] trade went over there to the new store. I noticed a difference, but gradually my customers came back because my prices are better. You see, that *Bok Guey* [white] also sells fried chicken and jojo potatoes. That's the kind of stuff the *Lo Mok* [blacks] go crazy over. We don't have that here, it's too much trouble and smells up the store."

"Were you afraid at first that he might pull all your business away?"

"I have to say yes, because business is tough these days for small stores like mine. It's not what it used to be back in my father's days. Then there was nobody but Chinese in the grocery business. Little by little the chain stores, supermarkets like Sunflower and Kroger, came along and took over. You see, their prices are better, and they deal in volume. Plus they have their own brands, and they can afford to sell cheaper than the Chi-

Businessmen claim to perform a necessary economic function for longtime black neighborhood customers who still buy on credit.

The Chinese grocery store also functions as a place for blacks to seek refuge from the hot sun, buy a cold drink, and socialize. In the past, the Chinese grocer helped blacks to interpret letters as well as provided a recruitment post for day laborers.

77

nese." Mr. Tong Mein lit his pipe and took a couple of puffs on it. Holding the bowl in his hand and pointing the stem at me, he continued. "You see, the *Lo Mok* [blacks] have food stamps and welfare money, and now they're thinking they are like white folk and can go into the big stores and shop like they do. You know, they squeeze the bread just like those white ladies you see on TV."

Moving away from the door, I watched a black man enter the store and approach the counter. Mr. Tong Mein slipped past me to wait on the customer.

"Hey, Charles, what do you want today?"

"Oh, I just come in to pay my bill today. I can't give you much 'cause my wife is sick and I got to carry her to the doctor. She's got high blood."

"Charles, I'm sorry to hear that. I hope she feels better tomorrow. You, okay, just give me what you can, and I'll carry you along. Don't worry none. I understand. . . . Say hi to Tassy for me."

The black man pulled out ten dollars and handed it to Mr. Tong Mein. "Thanks, and God bless you, T. M. I sure do appreciate your help."

As the man left, Mr. Tong Mein rang up the money and marked how much was received on a billing pad. On the spine of the pad, written in black ink, it read "Thomas, C." As he walked out from behind the counter he remarked, "Ole Charles has traded with me for a long time, and he always pays his bills on time."

I asked, "Does the *Bok Guey* [white] down the street give credit, too?"

"At first he didn't give credit, but then I heard he started to because he was losing business after a while. You know how the situation is with the *Lo Mok* [blacks]. There's lots of things that affect their income, such as the weather. When it's good and sunny they have work. And also the seasons. They don't have much work during the winter after everything's been harvested. So that guy down the street started giving credit, but he didn't know how much to give and who to give it to."

"Well, how do you know how much and who to give credit to?"

"Experience," he said. "You know something about the person, like who he is, what kind of job he has, who he knows, and what his ability to pay is. You ask questions and talk to them, and they'll tell you everything about themselves. Then over the years you get to know these guys, their pattern of buying and their ability to pay. That's how I learned."

"Then that *Bok Guey* [white] made a mistake in not knowing who to trust because he lacked the ability to deal with the *Lo Mok* [blacks]."

"That's right," responded Mr. Tong Mein, "Those other Chinese stores are hurting, too, and maybe they don't realize it. But the big Chinese stores do well and make lots of money. They will always survive in the Delta."

Businessmen told me that the owners of larger grocery stores in white neighborhoods employed a different business strategy from that of the Chinese who operated in the black community. Most customers in the former stores are white. Whites prefer a shopping atmosphere similar to that of large chain stores, with air conditioning, an abundance of space, lighting, packaged products, modern store fixtures, sale items, courteous service, gondola display, fresh produce and meats, and plenty of parking spaces. Chinese supermarkets provide these features. One businessman, the owner of a large store in a white neighborhood, commented on business strategy.

> I give the *Bok Guey* [whites] what they want if I am going to keep up with the *Bok Guey* chain stores. I specifically designed my store after the Sunflower grocery store. The food on the aisles follows the same pattern. All my meat and beverages and frozen food cases are modern and good-looking. The lights are soft white, which makes everything look good. The floors are always clean and waxed. My produce is fresh and crisp just like the *Bok Guey* [whites] like. I have USDA Choice meat, red and fresh. I tell my help to dress neat and clean and be courteous and friendly. I make sure they remember people's names and greet them when they come in. My sack clerks take groceries out to their cars and always say "Thank you for shopping." I have sales items all the time and put a big one-page ad in the newspaper on Wednesday. When something doesn't look right or smell right, I throw it away. My customers like to shop here because they get good service and good prices. That's my secret to winning, and I have done very well.

JACK'S STORE GOLD STAR A sharp contrast can be seen between the typical Chinese store located in the black neighborhood (above) and the modern Chinese store located in the white middle-class neighborhood (below).

Businessmen said they confronted a problem similar to that of the first generation in maintaining racial harmony. They have added to the repertoire of their fathers; for example, making monetary contributions to the whites and blacks (the Delta Citizens Council and the National Association for the Advancement of Colored People, or NAACP), eschewing overt political participation and listening with an attentive ear to both sides in order to gain understanding of the racial climate of opinion. One businessman who operates a self-service convenience and liquor store speaks of a capitalistic strategy, a position of vulnerability, and a way of remaining politically neutral:

I got good location in between the *Lo Mok* [blacks] and *Bok Guey* [Whites] on the highway. I did good business with both groups and saved my money to open up the package store. I figured that with my steady customers from the grocery business, they would also buy their liquor from me all in one trip. Well, I saved up my money and built an addition onto the store to sell liquor. It worked out just fine. My wife runs the grocery store and I run the liquor store. We're more accepted now than when my father ran the store a long time ago. But we still got to keep both sides happy, so I give to the *Hok Guey* [blacks] and *Bok Guey* [whites] charities and let them put posters every now and then in my store to advertise a community event. You still got to play it right, even though the Chinese are accepted in the Delta. That's the only way you're going to survive and make money. You could make a million dollars one day and lose it the next if you are in between like the Chinese people. It's a sticky situation, so you got to watch both the front door and the back door and don't offend anyone. The businessmen who can't do that don't survive.

They reported very little about what happened to merchants who failed to survive in the Delta—"they moved out of the Delta and started new business elsewhere." One businessman claimed that merchants who failed had lacked luck, industry, and the ability to deal with blacks.

I know of many businessmen who have failed and had to leave the Delta. But I'm not going to mention any names. Gosh, I've seen them come and go. If an older businessman fails, he moves out of the Delta to Houston or California to find a new start. Usually, he finds his relatives and borrows money from them to get started again. Nobody talks about people who don't make it, but word gets around. These guys who don't make it in the Delta start up new grocery stores or go into the restaurant business. Many people come here and think it's easy to live in the Delta, but they find out it's not so. They don't know how to handle the *Lo Mok* [blacks] because they're not used to these people. Some don't have enough "luck," either. They come here, buy a store, and have to raise three or four children and find out pretty soon they can't make it and have to pack up and leave. I tell you the truth, it's not easy here to make a living. ... Like my father used to say when he ran a grocery store: "success is one percent inspiration and ninety-nine percent perspiration." Well, he said it in Chinese. The main thing is you first have to learn how to handle blacks.

Businessmen at Church

Businessmen are Christians. Some attend church services regularly. Most go occasionally and insist that business keeps them away. They are members of one of the following churches: the Chinese Baptist church, the Chinese Baptist Mission, Methodist church, Presbyterian church, the Catholic church. Most are Baptists. Some older ones said they still held some traditional Chinese religious beliefs but refused to specifiy or discuss the contents of these beliefs. Most seem to have weaker religious commitments than old people. Many mentioned that churchgoing helps one socially and economically in the Delta milieu. The following statement by a merchant illustrates the point:

> Most of us businessmen belong to one kind of church or another. If you don't belong to a church, everyone around here wonders why. So many businessmen go to church to keep goodwill in the community. Some of those guys go to the *Bok Guey Yea Thlu Hong* [white church] in order to mix with the *Bok Guey* [whites], look good, and get more business. My wife and I still go, but not as much anymore. We work six long days a week, and so Sunday is our day of rest. Sometimes we go see our children on Sunday. Every now and then, if there's a big event at the Chinese church, we go, like during Christmas, Thanksgiving, and Easter. Or if someone gets married, we go. Most businessmen go every once in a while, but we got other things to do, too. It just depends on how much time you got and how much you believe in all that religious stuff. Religion is good for women and children. I'm still a Christian, but I still shoot off firecrackers in front of the store every Chinese New Year's to keep the evil spirits away. ... It can't hurt, you know.

Although some businessmen do not attend church on a regular basis, most insist that their wives and children go to church. Businessmen are proud of their wives' religious devotion and the regular church attendance of children. They also emphasize the religious activities of old people who set the course for Chinese activities in the Delta. One businessman's statement specifies the secular function of church and religion and stresses the importance of religion for women, children, and old people:

> Some businessmen are usually too busy to go to church, but the women have plenty of time. They read the Bible together and have refreshments at the church or at the preacher's house. They run the business meetings at the church. The women also plan the Sunday school activities for the children, and I think it's a good deal. Children must be taught the right ways. All of us realize how important the old people are. . . . I mean, they got the church going and helped the Chinese to be accepted in the Delta. and boy, they gave plenty of money to the Chinese church as well as to the Baptist churches so the *Bok Guey* [whites] would know we are, you know, Chinese instead of *Lo Mok.*

Businessmen cook for church suppers and wedding banquets. Wives prepare the rice, while men cook the main Chinese dishes. Men, skilled amateur chefs in their own right, prepare everything but roast pork and roast duck at nine-course wedding banquets.

Mr. Jom Gai said:

> I've cooked for many church dinners and wedding banquets over the years. Other businessmen like myself all help in preparing food for five to eight hundred people. It's a chore, let me tell you. The women distribute the rice cooking among themselves, say twenty or so women each have to cook twenty-five pounds of rice. The men cook all the Chinese dishes like sweet and sour chicken, chow mein, shrimp, beef chow yuke. Usually *sil jee* [roast pig] and *sil aup* [roast duck] are flown in from Los Angeles. We don't have the equipment to cook those things here. The cooking is a community effort. The businessmen work all the time and have no time to visit or talk, so when we cook, we all get together and visit at the same time. Everyone appreciates our efforts, and we don't mind doing it. They all tell us that the food tastes good, and that makes us feel great.

Businessmen serve as honorary or regular pallbearers at funerals in the Chinese community. They explain that because of

A mixture of western and traditional Chinese wedding customs is practiced in the Delta. A lovely Chinese bride dressed in a *kwa* (Chinese wedding gown), serves tea to her in-laws, thereby signifying her new status in her husband's family as well as socially bridging the two families via marriage.

The wedding banquet is a major festivity attended by hundreds of Chinese families throughout the Delta. White community leaders and prominent business people share in the celebration thus solidifying the social bond between the two groups. Four generations of Delta Chinese are seated at this table.

84

a dearth of Chinese men their age, they are often called upon for this task. Funerals in the Chinese community are similar in some respects to those of whites but retain some Chinese practices: for example, giving candy and *Lee Shee* (Chinese "lucky money") to mourners and providing a "longevity banquet" for mourners after the interment.[7]

Businessmen at Leisure

Businessmen said that their leisure time, usually Sundays, was spent driving to visit relatives or family, that is, their parents, brothers, sisters, in-laws, and grandchildren in and outside the Delta. The men enjoy fishing and hunting trips with sons and sons-in-law, while the women visit friends and relatives, chat, gossip, and shop for their grandchildren or children, all traditionally Southern forms of recreation. They entertain frequently at home, cooking Sunday afternoon dinners, hosting birthday and anniversary parties, observing Chinese and American holidays, and playing some family penny-ante poker. Some businessmen are invited to white poker games, but most decline these offers to mix because they desire to spend time with their families. Those few merchants who socialize with whites often belong to local community service organizations, the American Legion, and/or Veterans of Foreign Wars (VFW). A few spend leisure time on short family vacations to California or Texas, where they visit with relatives.

I often attended the Chinese Baptist Church of Cleveland and was usually invited to eat supper with some of the church members after the services. I was also frequently asked to the homes of businessmen throughout the Delta. These occasions afforded time for lengthy conversation concerning topics such as fishing, hunting, community life, gambling, and other leisure pursuits. The following excerpt is from a lengthier conversation with Mr. and Mrs. Yu Cheh, their college-aged daughter, Wanda, and their son, Benson, a high school student.

[7]For an ethnographic analysis of traditional Chinese funerary practices among Chinese Americans, see Robert S. Quan, "The Traditional Chinese Funerary Practices of Contemporary Pacific Coast Chinese Settlers in America," mimeographed (paper presented at the meeting of the Society for the Study of Symbolic Interactionism, San Francisco, September, 1978).

I asked Benson what he did with his leisure time. He replied, "Dad and I are fixing to go fishing next weekend."

"What kind of fishing do you guys do? Deep sea?"

"Bream fishing," Mr. Yu Cheh replied. "We go to the lake and rent a boat—get out there early in the morning when the fish are biting and catch perch, crappie, things like that."

I asked them if they did any hunting in the local area for deer, squirrel, rabbit, birds, or raccoons.

Mr. Yu Cheh replied, "I don't hunt, just like to fish. But Peter, my oldest son, and Ben used to go hunting a long time ago. This *Bok Guey* (white) friend, a real long-time friend, taught those guys how to hunt 'coons. He's a real nice man."

"What else do you do in your leisure time? Are you a member of any organizations?"

"Sure, my wife and I go down to the American Legion Hall once in a while to have some fun and talk to our friends. I'm a member down there."

Mrs. Yu Cheh, silent for a moment, now exclaimed, "Yeah, and the people at the *Bok Guey* [white] country club have invited us to come there!"

"That's very nice," I said.

Mr. Yu Cheh started laughing and apparently found humor in my statement. "Oh, ma, you don't want to go down to that country club. You'd get tired quick when those old *Hon Geng* ["rednecks"] start pawing all over you." Wanda and her brother burst out laughing, but Mrs. Yu Cheh said seriously: "We Chinese are a well-respected people in Mississippi. We've come a long ways. . . . People respect us." A moment of quiet hung in the air following her words.[8]

I directed my next question to Mrs. Yu Cheh "Do you play mah jongg at all? I've heard of some Chinese here playing mah jongg all night long."

"No!" she quickly replied. "We don't gamble, and we don't do those things in our family. But I tell you there are some Chinese who like to play mah jongg a whole lot. It gets to be a habit with them. . . . They can't quit."

[8]In nearly every conversation, the Delta Chinese of the first two generations spoke of the respect shown them by the whites. Such emphasis may mean that some Chinese have doubts as to how the whites feel about them.

Her husband added, "And there are some Chinese business-men who play poker with the *Bok Guey* [whites], but they don't like to play for big stakes. If the *Bok Guey* loses a thousand bucks, that's nothing compared to that much for a small mer-chant like the Chinese. That's foolishness."

Our conversation had taken place during a short trip by car, and we now drew up to Ben's aunt's house. A gray-haired little old lady smiled at us from the front porch.

Such trips are not frequent. Most businessmen prefer to stay at home with the family. One man remarked:

> My wife and I usually stay home on our days off. That's if we're not going to a wedding or something like that. Our oldest children drive up to see us from Jackson. Our youngest son is married and lives in Memphis, and he comes down with his wife now and then. My wife fixes supper, and we all sit around together to talk for hours or maybe watch a ball game. We take off on Sundays be-cause of the store. But my cousin, Chuin Gen, has a restaurant, and he closes on Monday. That's one thing I don't have to do is slave over a hot stove like he does. . . . I can relax.

Businessmen in the Triethnic Community

Businessmen work to perpetuate the Chinese community created by their predecessors, now the old people. These mer-chants said they were accepted by blacks and whites because they belonged to a Christian church, practiced endogamy, fol-lowed the Chinese way, taught their children how to get along with whites and blacks, deferred to whites, and avoided racial conflict, especially during the 1960s civil rights era. Business-men recognize that Rev. Martin Luther King's efforts to estab-lish racial equality for blacks in the South have also helped the Delta Chinese in their quest for social acceptance. Businessmen note with some anxiety that the traditional pattern of race rela-tions existing between whites and blacks and between Chinese and blacks has changed. They report that some young blacks today are militant and litigious political activists. Grocery mer-chants located in black neighborhoods confront a more prob-lematic situation in maintaining racial harmony than do the few Chinese businessmen who operate businesses in the white com-munity. Merchants delare that in order to get along with whites and blacks they have to "Watch their step" with blacks more carefully than in the past. They imply that it is not as easy now to manage black customers as it was before the 1960s. Some are anxious about the blacks' push upward because they feel themselves to be the group in the middle, the group that may be squeezed. On the other hand most voice agreement with the civil rights movement.

The grocery merchants, restauranteurs, and shopkeepers located in the white community deal mostly with whites and with blacks, in their words, "a cut above the rest of the *Lo Mok* [blacks] and the 'rednecks." Moreover these businessmen, unlike old people, interact frequently in a friendly fashion with white customers at their places of business.

They hold that belonging to the "right" church, maintaining Chinese marriages, staying away from intimate social contacts with blacks, and showing whites they are a distinctive people are measures necessary for the maintenance of the Chinese community. One merchant's account supported this strategy:

> Businessmen like myself carry out most of the burden in keeping the Chinese community going in the Delta. Most of the old people are retired, so it's our duty to keep the water calm and clear, if you know what I mean. We don't have any social contacts with blacks. We go to the Baptist Church because that is what most of us are. In other words if you don't belong to a church, the *Bok Guey* [whites] don't think you are a good citizen . . . or your family either. We hold big weddings when our Chinese people get married. We invite our *Bok Guey* [white] friends to come and celebrate with us. We want to show them that we are Chinese. They come to our banquet, and we show them the richness of the Chinese heritage. We always see to it that the mayor or some of the *dai pow* ["big shots"] come to have dinner with us. Some even make a little speech, and that's real nice. We appreciate it. You see, we want to let everyone know that, "Hey, we're proud to be Chinese."

I found in interviews with whites that churchgoing among the Delta Chinese was related to their acceptance by the white community as Chinese. One white offered the following typical comments:

> If it hadn't been for the church, the Chinese wouldn't have been as well accepted as they are today. The Chinese are church mem-

bers and good respectable people in the community. If they didn't go to church, most people wouldn't trust them. Somebody that doesn't go to church and pay his respect to the Lord is not a real honest and sincere person. These Chinese are sincere in their worship as they are in the other aspects of their lives. They are a well-kept group of people who live right and are respected. They are different from blacks.

Businessmen teach their children to respect everyone in order to avoid racial conflict. Mr. Ho Lai commented:

> When my children are young, we teach them at home to be nice to everyone. We tell them to call grownups "mister," "sir," "miz," and "mam." If our children don't learn respect, they aren't going to get it in return. That way we don't get no trouble, you see. They watch the way we act toward the *Bok Guey* [whites], and they learn pretty quick what's right.

One white merchant remarked on the Chinese people's sense of etiquette: "When I go to Ho's he is always friendly and greets me like he hasn't seen me for ages. His children are very disciplined and have good manners. I wish everyone was as nice as that family. They all know how to act right. We respect that in him. He raised some decent children."

Businessmen remember the 1960s civil rights era and how they weathered the storm by making political contributions to insure their own security. Although in a few incidents blacks were reported to have thrown bricks and set small fires, the Chinese merchants did not perceive these actions as racially oriented. They claimed that it was "just a few *Lo Mok* letting off some steam." One businessman said of the racial situation in Greenville during the civil rights period:

> Greenville is a liberal town, and during the height of Martin Luther King the colored people didn't want trouble, so they told him not to come. The Chinese gave money privately to help the blacks and black politicians. You know, we donated to the NAACP, black athletic clubs, and black churches. There were no damage to Chinese businesses, and we weren't worried because we knew most of the blacks. They respected us.

Businessmen also talked about the growing acceptance of the Chinese in the Delta since Dr. Martin Luther King's efforts to establish racial equality. They know that the Chinese did not engage in any overt activities conducive to the civil rights movement, a movement which brought some change in the Delta race relations. One merchant declared:

> The Chinese in *Nam Fong* [the South] have come a long way. We worked ourselves up from the bottom. We appreciated Reverend King's efforts to help the colored people. Because when he helped them, he also helped us, the Chinese, in becoming accepted in the Delta. He was a great man, yes, he was. He made the *Bok Guey* [whites] realize that a person is a human being with work to do and a family to feed no matter what color he is. Reverend King was a real Christian man and we all respect him. When he was shot in Memphis all the Chinese businessmen were a little worried the *Lo Mok* [blacks] would go crazy or something and burn us all down just to spite everyone, but they didn't. No matter what we do, we're caught in the middle.

The blacks expressed an uneven, mixed view of businessmen and other Chinese. Some, particularly young adults, portrayed Chinese merchants as clannish exploiters who played the white man's racial game to make money from blacks. Others saw them as friendly modest merchants despite their affluence. Still others viewed them as a separate race caught in the middle. Blacks generally respect the Chinese because they are successful and because they treat blacks with respect. One black commented:

> The Mississippi Chinese regardless of how successful they are don't forget where they come from. They had to work hard to earn respect from the white man. I'm sure that they have relatives in other places they have to support. From what I see, they're people who don't let success go to their heads. They prove they been blessed. They give blacks an even chance to life. They gives a helping hand. They be friendly people most time. They make money off us, but what can you 'spect. . . .

Businessmen say that before the civil rights movement they could exercise some authority over blacks they caught shoplifting. They often spanked a child caught stealing and called his mother. The paternalistic system has passed. One may not strike a young thief today without chancing legal action as well as business losses. One businessman deplores the changing times:

> Today things ain't like what they used to be in the past. The *Lo Mok* [blacks] were easier to get along with back then, say fifteen

years ago. I remember one time I caught these two *Hok Guey Doy* [black male children]. One was trying to steal a can of tuna fish. The other was opening up boxes of cereal trying to get the toys out. You know, usually I'd have one of my children follow the *Lo Mok* around the store so this kind of thing wouldn't happen. . . . But anyway, I caught them two boys, took them out back and whupped their butts. They were so scared they wouldn't tell no one. Then I called their mother and told her what happened. She appreciated it and told me to teach them a lesson. You know, I was giving them credit in those days and they didn't want to be dropped. Now it's different—you touch one of them, and they raise all kind of hell, call the NAACP, take you to court, boycott your store. . . . It ain't worth it. It's better striking a *Bok Guey* [white] than a *Hok Guey* [black]. The times have changed, ain't what it used to be.

One incident in the community involved a black boycott of a Chinese grocery store. Mrs. Fannie Brookins, boycott leader and the mother of a nine-year-old, charged grocer Don Quon of Indianola with striking her son during a May 26, 1978, dispute over a purchase.[9] Though Brookins maintained that Quon privately admitted to having struck her son, Nelson Brookins, he refused to make a public apology. Quon swore innocence during a June 12 trial and was acquitted of an assault charge. The Indianola NAACP chapter boycotted Quon's grocery after Quon asked Judge Hamilton for a court order barring the Brookins family from his store. Brookins would not agree to a legal compromise but instead wanted Quon to apologize to the whole black neighborhood at an open NAACP meeting—to show, in her words, "that I am not a liar and my child is not a liar." Shortly afterward Brookins received an anonymous postcard proclaiming the merits of the Chinese people and pleading for Brookins to stop persecuting Quon. Mrs. Brookins's determination increased: "And I don't have any pity at all for Don. He can sit in that store and rot. We will be outside till he does."

Businessmen reported to me many incidents of the 1960s which indicated that the Delta's racial climate and pressure were changing. One store owner recalled white pressure:

[9] David Saltz, "Public Apology Still Demanded," *Delta Democrat Times,* August 5, 1978, p. 1.

At one time I remember in Indianola in the 1960s when the blacks were boycotting the white merchants. Ho Toy's store had just opened up, and at first he didn't have much business. But when the boycott happened, all the colored people went over to his store because it was one of the biggest stores in town. He got all this business and made lots of money. So he started donating to the NAACP. What do you know, pretty soon the whites wanted him to donate to the White Citizens Council. So he had to give them some money too in order to stay in business. When he did that, he didn't get no more trouble.

A knowledgeable white insider recalled a situation involving two white factions that demanded donations in the late 1960s from Chinese businessmen: "There was another grocer up the Delta who was caught in a bad situation. He was giving contributions to one white group, and there was a power struggle that ended up in a split. When the other group got into power, he had to give them money, too."

Businessmen recognize class difference among blacks as well as whites. To them middle-class blacks are more educated, economically stable, mannerly, and moral than lower-class blacks and on this basis deserve more respect and better service. All people are respected, but some are more respectable and respected than others.

I talked with Mr. Gee Fon at his Chinese restaurant one late evening. The discussion eventually turned to race relations in the Delta.

I said, "You know, every time I come here to eat, I seldom notice any *Lo Mok.*"

Mr. Gee Fon shook his head. "No, the *Lo Mok* [blacks] hardly ever come in here to eat. Sometimes some of them come from the university. Other times some high-class *Lo Mok* stop in. Usually those people are passing through town, or they are ministers or school teachers. Some work for the university. Those kind of *Lo Mok* are a cut above the rest of their people. They are friendly, and I treat them good, like the rest of my customers."

"You know," I said, "the Chinese store owners in *Hok Guey Fao* [black community] tell me they have to watch their step so as to get along."

"That's right," replied Mr. Gee Fon. "I have a cousin in Greenville that owns a store in *Hok Guey Fao,* and he's got to treat the *Lo Mok* right, or they'll go to another store and shop. He's dealing with the lower class there but making out all right. He can handle them, and that's what it takes. My customers are respectable people who don't like trouble, and I don't either, but down there you got a lot more problems to deal with than over on this side. It's not easy anywhere, but I think high-class people are more educated and easier to get along with." A moment later, leaving my table, Mr. Gee Fon cheerfully escorted a white middle-aged couple to the far end of the dining room. Obviously he enjoyed his position in the business community.

Though most businessmen are apolitical (at least overtly), some showed active political interests within certain restricted contexts. When I asked them about Mayor John Wing of Jonestown, they were willing to talk about the Chinese in Delta politics. They said the Chinese had a chance of winning political offices in small Delta towns where blacks and whites were approximately equal in numbers because in such situations they could play intermediate political roles. One businessman explained: "In small towns, the Chinese are right in the middle of the blacks and the whites. Because they're neutral and fair, they prevent both sides from fighting over power. They satisfy both sides and make everyone happy."[10]

Businessmen understand that the traditional patterns of race relations have broken down and that consequently they, the blacks, and the whites face a problematic situation in this area. They also realize that inevitable further changes will require ongoing negotiations and a persistent jockeying for position.

Businessmen define themselves in terms of three major role identities: successful merchants, good family men, and Delta Chinese. Self-styled disciplinarians, they advocate respect for elders and others and promote education and endogamy in their children. Businessmen also view themselves as helpful and

[10]For an interesting article on a Chinese mayor in the Delta, see Dan Henderson, "The Inscrutable Mayor of Turrel," *Mid-South Magazine* of the *Memphis Commercial Appeal,* July 24, 1977, pp. 4–6

friendly merchants to their customers, compromisers as the group in between in race relations, philanthropists who contribute to black and white organizations, and powerful leaders in the Delta Chinese community.

Similar in certain respects to their predecessors in the first generation, businessmen perceive the world as a competitive marketplace in which they have to create their own existence and provide for their children's social and economic welfare. Their world, however, is a larger, more complex and more interrelated marketplace than that of their fathers. The Delta has expanded, and some foresee a further expansion for their children. Businessmen have widened their perspective as they have ventured from the black community to compete with the white merchants in white territories. They must transact business like white men in a white man's world. Businessmen state that the times are changing and that their children's views will be wider than theirs, just as theirs are wider than those of old people. They told me that their children had to learn the American way as well as the Chinese way in order to achieve success.

The individuals with whom I spoke underscored the necessity to maintain a working relationship with both blacks and whites while simultaneously seeking wealth and status—which as capitalists they desire and which as minority group members they treasure as security. One merchant disclosed a scenario which typified the world view of businessmen:

> I see that to make it in this world you've got to be able to walk free of conflict and violence. You have to be respected on both sides of the street. I teach my children these things, especially to be polite and to behave. I don't want my family to have a bad name with the *Lo Fan* [whites] or the *Lo Mok* [blacks]. Being in the middle is like walking on a thin line, but you got to play up to the big-shot whites. You can't stay completely in the middle. You've got to attend to both sides and know what is going on. The work is not easy, and that's why I tell my children to study hard and get a good job and get away from this kind of work. That's better for them to do than what I'm doing. The pace is slow for me, but I'm patient. My children don't see the world like I see it. But they'll make it because I see to it that they learn all they can from me the stuff that's not written in the books about how to live and survive in the Delta. Over the years now I've grown used to

it, maybe more tolerant of its changes. The ones who couldn't tolerate it left.

Obviously the businessman's world view is much more Americanized than that of first-generation members. He knows that the third generation is leaving the Delta and that the outmigration process is accelerating.

Businessmen's View of Other Community Groups
Old People

Businessmen describe old people as their dear respected parents, friends, and relatives. They pointed out that the first generation taught them the Chinese way and had paved the way for their success. On the other hand, they recognize that they are much more Americanized than their parents and that succeeding generations will be even more Americanzed than they are. One merchant explained:

> We have a lot in common with the old people, the way we see the world and the way we must live to survive in this world. We respect them for their teaching, but they think the world today can still run by the old ways, and that is not true. They live too much in the past. See, things change awfully quick, and we got to change with it. When the *Lo Mok* didn't make much money and had no transportation, they bought groceries mainly from the Chinese merchants. We gave them credit and carried them for years. Now with more welfare the younger generations of *Lo Mok* are *sa cheen* [ostentatious]. They can go other places to buy food. I used to sell hardware way back, but I had to quit because the hardware stores moved in. You have to change with the times. Not much left for the future of the stores because none of my children want to run it. They're all becoming professionals. That's how fast things are changing, and they're not hung up on the Chinese ways either.

Businessmen think old people see them as industrious, determined, frugal, self-sacrificing sons who have provided well for their families—and who for the most part have followed the Chinese way.

Professionals

Businessmen, unlike the old people, accept the mixed blessings that accompany their children's professional and social

95

status. They are proud that the professionals have "outdistanced" them, that is, that they have reached a higher educational and social level and have won greater recognition in the wider community. Businessmen note that professionals do not have to worry about blacks or about "hustling" to make money as they themselves do. Moreover, they evidence a matter-of-fact understanding of the professional's partial break with traditional Chinese ways. One proud merchant father commented on the success, Americanization, and Chinese group membership of his children:

> All of my sons are professionals, and I have one daughter who is a pharmacist. I practically own part of Ole Miss for putting all of my children through college there. At college they mix with the *Bok Guey* [whites], and they begin to think like them. There's not too much Chinese in them, but they might tell you differently. But they're not white, they're not colored or black either, thank God. I can't really blame them because you got to look toward the future. They are successful, have high-paying jobs and are happy. That makes me happy too. As much as I'd like them to stay around home, I know they must go somewhere else to find a decent job. Just so long as they come home and visit me once in a while. I wanted them to make it—have an education, not to be like me and have to sweat it out each day. I'm proud of them. They can give their children the things I couldn't give to my children when we were struggling to make it. They won't have to work long hours in the store and put up with blacks. As long as they stay here they got to be Chinese. There's nothing else to be.

Businessmen assume that professionals picture them as frugal, respected, wise, experienced, parents who follow both the Chinese and American way, winners who still can give good advice to younger generations.

College Students

Businessmen said that the college student category included their children. They claim to influence at home this group's behavior with reference to dress, manners, religion, and sexuality. They admitted, however, that they know little about the behavior and thinking of this generation at college or beyond the home. They say that most made good grades and that all pass. As parents they fear that these students live a secret independent life while away from home and that they behave in the

American way. Businessmen hope the students will "stay out of trouble" and "avoid sexual difficulty." They realize that this third generation will inevitably become more assimilated than they themselves have. One businessman assessed college students and suggested that they were looking for new identities:

> We're proud of our college students who do well in school. They make us very happy by making good grades and winning awards. That's because we taught them to be disciplined. The college students want to become professional people, and they are starting to think and act like them. I know that I don't have much to say when they leave home. I just hope they don't run around with the wrong kind of people and get in trouble. With my oldest son, who is an accountant, he had more Chinese *lai mau* [manners] than one of my younger sons. Those two guys are so different, like day and night. Ma and I realize that it can't be helped. The younger generation is not very Chinese anymore. But that's okay as long as they are successful. Then maybe they'll discover who they really are. . . .

Businessmen think college students love and respect them as parents but at the same time consider them to be old-fashioned and stubborn.

Young People

Businessmen described members of this group as their younger children and grandchildren. Young people are required to participate in Chinese community activities, where they come into contact with old people, Chinese peers, and other members of the Chinese community. Businessmen claim that they and their wives see to it that the young people develop a sense of respect and reverence for elders. Businessmen are happy about the way young people conduct themselves and consider them the wave of the future. Mr. Seem Hee commented about this group:

> The young people are a source of happiness in the Chinese community. They are confident, well mannered, disciplined, and got a lot going for them. The young people in high school make good grades and become leaders in their class. The ones on the way up help out their families at home, church, and in the family business. We give them everything we can: love, money and security, because they are the only hope for carrying on some of the Chinese traditions that we are proud of here in the Delta. They will be a

97

very successful group because they have learned from those before them, their grandparents, brothers, sisters, and us.[11]

Businessmen think young people view them as hard-working, warm, friendly, loving fathers, uncles, and grandfathers.

Women

To businessmen the old women are headstrong, traditional, industrious providers for their children and perpetuators of Chinese culture in the Delta. Merchants appreciate them as respected mothers, aunts, elders, and helpers over the years in the grocery stores. One businessman characterized the position of old women in the Chinese community.

> Without the old women the Chinese would not have made much headway in Mississippi. They took care of their families and helped other families. They taught their children the right things and the Chinese way. We honor and respect them for their kindness of heart, strong character, and wisdom. They have worked hard through the years raising children, working in the stores, and running the Chinese church. The old women hold a special spot in the hearts of all Chinese people.

Businessmen believe that old women define them as industrious, frugal sons and friends who still remember the first generation and the hard times. They also think the first generation appreciates their help in interpreting the American way.

Businessmen look upon young married women as their daughters, relatives, and their friends' daughters. They are modern, independent, self-assertive, educated mothers and future mothers who are a source of pride and happiness. Businessmen agree with old people that this group possesses a hybrid Delta Chinese identity mixed with an American identity. They reported that most of these women married well; that is, mar-

[11]Some businessmen still observe the traditional Chinese *Hone Aun* [red egg] party to celebrate a newborn son. Red eggs, symbolic of a new baby in the family, are traditionally supposed to insure a long, happy life for the new infant. This celebration is important because the male child carries on the family name, and so family members and friends are invited to share in the happiness. Gold jewelry imported from Hong Kong is given to the one-month-old infant. In the case of Mr. and Mrs. Johnny Choo, their new son, Jeffrey, is already a 10 percent owner of Bing's Food Store, the family business. For further information on this traditional Chinese celebration, see Lynn Walcott, "Red Egg Party Celebrates Birth," *Delta-Democrat Times,* July 24, 1977, p. 23.

ried Chinese professionals or businessmen. One merchant praised this group:

> The young married women today are financially secure because most of them got a good education and married good Chinese men. Some of them have professional training as schoolteachers and pharmacists. They can work part time and still raise their children. We're all very proud of them and their success shows that they are educated and hard working. They often do things their way because they're modern, but they don't forget the Chinese ways they grew up with. We look at them as our hope for the future, a new crop of better educated Chinese people.

One may wonder about the probability of unreported negative cases, about those who did not achieve success, marry professionals, or marry Chinese men. I probed in this area but did not find many representative cases. Businessmen assume that young married women love them as respected, generous parents, relatives, and friends, and as frugal, industrious men who keep the Chinese community alive in the Delta.

Businessmen described young unmarried women as the most independent and Americanized Chinese group. Merchants hope that these educated and outspoken young women will eventually find a more consistent identity after getting married. Businessmen, like old people, believe that young women should marry after college and should not forgo marriage for a career. They are resigned to the fact that some young unmarried women pursue a professional or work career prior to marriage. One businessman spoke about this group:

> The young unmarried women in the Chinese community will eventually marry and settle down. But right now they're still trying to establish themselves. They are very bright and educated and have made up their minds about what they're going to do in life. They are very independent and want a career instead of a marriage. I tell my daughter that she can have both, but she's already made up her mind. It takes a little time before she sees what I mean. I think she'll do all right and come out okay. She will have to decide whoever it is she wants to be. And she's going to marry whoever she wants to. What can I do about that?

Businessmen believe young unmarried women see them as respected, prosperous, helpful, well-loved parents, relatives, and friends who lack a clear understanding of what a professional career entails for a female. My observation and reports suggest that this belief is correct.

The Professionals

Professionals hold the third position in the Delta Chinese community's deference hierarchy. With parents who are now old people and businessmen in the Delta, they range in age from the mid-twenties to the mid-forties. Professionals form a group of educated, successful, and mobile people. The Chinese community defines a professional as anyone with a college degree who has a good white-collar job. This group includes bank employees, business managers, bookkeepers, accountants, sales managers, insurance salesmen, radio-television personnel, computer scientists, commercial artists, and personnel clerks. Some Chinese are also teachers, chemists, nurses, architects, engineers, pharmacists, professors, and medical technicians. Most are accountants, business managers, pharmacists, and engineers. Very few enter the humanities because, as they put it, "that's not where the money is." Most are educated at either the University of Mississippi in Oxford or Mississippi State University in Starkville, Mississippi.

Pharmacists and accountants find work in Mississippi near their families. Some of them work in family businesses. Others, because of a dearth of job opportunities in the Delta, go elsewhere in the South to such places as Atlanta, Baton Rouge, New Orleans, Houston, and Memphis. Delta Chinese outmigrants are developing communities in Jackson, Mississippi, and Memphis, Tennessee. Many graduate engineers move to Houston, a large industrial city which sustains a Chinese-American community whose membership comes primarily from the Mississippi Delta. A few professionals claimed no desire to live and work in the South and sought positions in New York, Los Angeles, and San Francisco, cities with sizable Chinese-American populations. These few constitute the most mobile professional group.

Professionals reflect their merchant middle-class socioeconomic background. They grew up as Delta Chinese with the Southern Baptist religion. All exhibit Delta Chinese cultural traits in language, speech patterns, religion, diet, customs, mannerisms, and attitude toward race relations. Most worked in Delta Chinese grocery stores while they were children, and most learned in the Delta how to get along with blacks and whites. All are heavily indoctrinated with the Protestant work ethic and its ramifications for education, religion, leisure, morals, and capitalism. Most are moving up to Southern upper-middle-class status attitudinally and culturally, if not financially.

I observed that professionals spoke English at the worksite and a combination of Southern English and Cantonese at home and when they were with Chinese-speaking people in other settings. Those under thirty speak very little Cantonese. Most, especially those over thirty, practice endogamous marriage, choosing as mates Delta Chinese Mississippians of similar social class background. Professionals claim that the Chinese prohibition against marriage to a person with the same surname has been breached occasionally in the Delta, though with no apparent negative consequences. Professionals as well as members of other groups reported efforts to avoid marriage with anyone of the same surname. Many professionals told me that the Delta Chinese population included only a few major family-named clans—all kin to each other. Therefore, professionals explained, they sought marriage partners outside the Delta. Still, I observed that Delta Chinese married Delta Chinese, though not close relatives. Isolation in rural areas and small towns has been responsible for this phenomenon. Cousin marriages were common in the antebellum South among the planter class as a means of keeping land in the family. Cousin marriages have decreased in the South since Reconstruction but do occur, though the couple involved is frequently unaware of the family connection at the time of the wedding. The old, small-town Southern saying that "all the white folks in town look alike" probably has some genetic foundation.

Professionals reported that those few Chinese professionals who intermarried with whites currently reside outside the Delta. They said they were freer from parental pressure in mate selection than were nonprofessional groups because of their success and financial independence. Professionals prefer to marry within their race, but some seek other mates when they fail to find suitable Chinese mates. Parents exert heavy pressure on most of them to get married as soon as they finish school. Younger professionals insist on making their own mate selections and say that "old-fashioned minds" have no place in this area. I noticed that professionals usually married with parental consent.

Professionals live in attractive upper-middle-class apartments and houses and drive expensive, late-model cars. Annual incomes range from $12,000 to $50,000. Most dress in middle-class style and wear expensive Chinese jewelry. Professionals travel on business and pleasure trips in and outside the South. Outside the South they find themselves different from other Chinese Americans in religion, diet, looks, customs, and speech patterns. Most prefer the Delta to the places they visit outside the South. They evince a secure, self-assured mien and talk frequently about making and investing money, as do many other American professionals.

Professionals at Home

Professionals form for the most part a modern, affluent, educated group of parents and homeowners. Their living accommodations reflect an upper-middle-class life-style. Homes are located in middle-class residential areas. Interior decors follow contemporary American design, and modern furniture and appliances are available. Professionals over age thirty-five display in their homes oriental objects such as pieces of Chinese furniture and wall hangings, oriental rugs, and China porcelain vases. They say these objects symbolize a Chinese cultural past and enable them to accentuate an ethnic affiliation in a tasteful, expensive fashion. The homes of many younger professionals contain fewer Chinese symbols. In most professional homes one sees professional identity objects such as journals, other occupational reading materials, and various artifacts (a pharmacist might have a mortar and pestle collection). The living rooms are filled with expensive furniture, though such rooms are used infrequently.

Professionals spend time at home reading newspapers, popular magazines, and books and journals in their fields. They are responsive to the media and appreciate rhythm and blues, popular music, the movies, and television. One pharmacist talked about spending time at home:

> I like to read the newspaper so I know about the current events. I like to collect books and records. Also, I subscribe to a number of journals to keep abreast of new developments in my field. There's always something new to learn about. But don't get me wrong. I'm not a bookworm. I like to entertain, cook, and try out new recipes on my friends. And I like to watch TV and listen to music.

Professionals are extroverted pragmatic people who enjoy gourmet cooking and throwing parties. They invite family members as well as some professional associates and friends from the white community on these festive occasions. Conversations cover a variety of topics during these social gatherings, including shoptalk and everyday events. Most talk is relaxed and conversational, encompassing gossip, real estate, sports, cars, the weather, local events, the movies, clothes, food, agricultural crops, real estate, and anecdotes or jokes. Professionals frequently tell jokes to reaffirm their professional status as well as their Chinese identity, an identity they can now afford to be proud of and joke about. I listened to the following dialogue between two Chinese professionals and a white professional couple at a party:

"Do you know what a Chonky is?" Sam asked the white couple.

"No. Tell us what a Chonky is."

"A Chinese honkey." There were chuckles throughout the group. "How about a Chippie, do you know what that is? A Chinese hippie!" This joke brought another wave of laughter, which continued as the white man traded jokes.

John, a Chinese professional, offered a more provocative joke about the social interaction between a Chinese patron and a black bartender at a night club. "There was a Chinese man who walked into this bar and sat down. He said to the bartender, 'Give me a Jack Daniels on the rocks, boy!' The drink was delivered and the Chinese customer finished it and ordered another in the same fashion. 'Give me a Jack Daniels on the rocks, boy!' This time the irritated black bartender replied, 'I don't like you calling me boy, boy. How would you like to be in my place?' The Chinese customer agreed to change places. As he put on an apron and took his place behind the bar, the black man walked outside, came back in, and took a seat at the bar and said, 'Give me a Jack Daniels on the rocks, boy!' The Chinese bartender looked askance at the black man and exclaimed, 'We don't serve niggers here!' "[1]

John's joke filled the room with mirth and apparent solidarity. The white couple poured John some more wine and toasted him for being such a good raconteur. Chinese professionals at such mixed parties reaffirm their solidarity with whites. The whites play along. Both sets of actors know the game and the roles and script that go along with it. Whites are at the top of the Delta social system; the Chinese come second and are moving up; the blacks are still on the bottom. Professionals tell another set of jokes to exclusively Chinese audiences and sometimes tell deprecating jokes about whites and blacks to one another.

Professionals frequently marry other professionals (or mates with college degrees) and have three of four children—a large family, especially for American professionals generally. They are lenient and indulgent in socializing their young, though they indoctrinate them with middle-class cultural values, for example, the importance of good grades, music, dancing (children receive lessons), religion, etiquette, and proper social behavior. Children's toys are educational, and they are not often permitted to play school sports. Professionals insist that their children use any extra time for study, schoolwork, or activities

---

[1]The best ethnic jokes are often told by members of the group concerned. Individuals rarely denigrate members of other ethnic groups to their face with jokes about them. This joke depends (in both form and content) on the Southern white ideology in which young Chinese professionals find themselves immersed.

that lead to social advancement. In this last attitude, again, they are similar to middle-class whites.

Single professionals usually live in rented apartments, and their life-style resembles that of other middle-class Americans. I noted few Chinese objects or symbols in their dwellings. Single professional women seemed to be more independent generally and less dependent on their parents than were single male professionals.

Professionals at Work

Professionals are skillful, serious, and diligent at the worksite. All of those I talked to appeared to be satisfied with their occupational careers. They are recognized by colleagues, the Chinese community, and the wider community as capable within their callings. One of them remarked to me:

> I am a pharmacist, and I have to perform my job with the utmost precision. A mistake could ruin my reputation and other people's lives. Some people think that pharmacy is like the grocery business, except it's more lucrative. That's not quite true. Pharmacy takes years of training before we can be licensed. I am a serious professional, and everyone sees me that way. I am respected in the community by whites, blacks, and Chinese, they know me as Sue the pharmacist, not the Chinese pharmacist.

Few professionals have employment problems. Pharmacists and accountants reported that job opportunities were always open in the Delta. Many engineers (particularly chemical and petroleum engineers) move to southern Mississippi, Louisiana, and Texas for positions. Professionlas reported that work opportunities had recently presented themselves in health and laboratory technology. This group claimed that law, politics, and medicine were dominated by Caucasians. Few showed any serious interest in law or politics, but many expressed keen interests in medicine. Some children of professionals will probably go to medical school; they are ambitious, they desire to be professionals, and their parents have the money to send them. Female professionals follow the occupational patterns of their male counterparts. However, more women than men are engaged in teaching, nursing, medical technology, and office jobs. They appear as dedicated to their work roles as the males.

The professionals are not interested in agriculture or agribusiness, though educational and career opportunities are open in these areas in Mississippi. Instead they lean toward business and technical fields. I heard very little from the professionals about blue-collar workers. How many Chinese have taken or will take blue-collar jobs remains unknown.

Professionals at Church

Professionals are Christian Baptists who say they have been "saved" and baptized. All go to church, some regularly, some now and then. All expect their wives and children to attend church regularly. Those over thirty-five attend church services more often than those younger. Some said they went to church to please their parents and the old people and for the sake of the children. Others claimed they attended for religious, social, work, and professional reasons. (In this respect they are similar to middle-class white Southerners.) Professionals participate in church activities less frequently than their parents, but all appear to be true believers.

None practices Chinese religions, though older professionals are somewhat familiar with ancestor worship, which they prefer to call "ancestor respect."

This statement by an accountant illustrates the professionals' religious orientation:

> Most all Chinese professionals I know are Christians and attend churches sometimes throughout the Delta. Most of us are Southern Baptist because that was what we were brought up on. As Christians we are highly respected in the greater community and stick to our Christian beliefs. We don't believe in Chinese religion. They worship idols and things like that. We believe in only one God and Jesus Christ.[2]

I found the professionals to be somewhat less religious than their parents. The age factor could explain this difference; as

[2] Interviews disclosed that this community group lacked knowledge of any Chinese religion. Its religious values reflect the dominant Southern white culture.

the professionals become older, their attitudes may change. Professionals in all ethnic groups tend to be more secularized than individuals who earn a living in other ways.

Professionals at Leisure

Professionals are more versatile in leisure activities than businessmen or old people. They also have more time to visit, travel, and entertain. Professionals visit with family, relatives, and friends in the Delta and make weekend trips to Memphis, Jackson, Houston, and the Mississippi Gulf Coast. They entertain Chinese and white friends at home and visit in white homes. A few claimed to be outdoor sports enthusiasts who enjoyed tennis, boating, water skiing, fishing, and hunting, but to my knowledge only a very few engaged in sports other than hunting and fishing.

One pharmacist's remarks about her visit to California and San Francisco's Chinatown, which I overheard at a party, were similar to those other Chinese had made in my presence on many occasions. They demonstrate that the Delta Chinese are Southerners in speech patterns, syntax, rhythm, repetition, phraseology, expectations, and provincial point of view.

I got the biggest surprise of my life, honey, when we hit 'Frisco. We visited the zoo and the park, and the museum and Fisherman's Wharf and we rode the trolley cars. Then, when we hit Chinatown, I was floored to see so many thousands of Chinese. I mean laid out, girl. And they all looked alike. It was so crowded. I couldn't breathe. I mean they were everywhere—back of me, in front of me, to the side and under my feet. I didn't feel comfortable—there were too many of them. We went to a bar to get a drink, and what do I run into? More Chinese again. They all looked like they had just gotten off the boat! The Chinese there were shorter, skinnier, and lighter. They dressed and acted different from us Chinese in the Delta. They talked and moved too fast. They all wanted to sit so close to one another—all over each other and talking and spitting on each other. I thought, give me space, God! They talked funny in different dialects—anyway, I couldn't understand them. It was a strange experience. I don't think I'll ever go back there again. It's too much on my heart, child, you know what I mean. Those Chinese were foreigners, girl. You know what I mean . . ., funny looking foreigners.

Other Southerners note the lack of space and the way it is utilized outside the rural South. Southerners do not like either to sit too close together or to talk in each other's faces. They are also used to people who look alike, talk alike, think alike, act alike, dress alike, and move and walk in similar fashion. Of course, there are class differences in all of these traits, but certain broad similarities seem to transcend class and even racial differences.

Professionals in the Triethnic Community

Professionals claim few social contacts with blacks because of their occupations and "social relations." By "social relations" they mean social contacts made on the basis of class and race. Pharmacists, teachers, and others who come in contact with a broad public deal with blacks and whites of all social classes. Though the professionals, like the businessmen, negotiate with all classes and races at an impersonal economic level, their work environments are different. The Chinese grocer exercises ultimate control over his customers because he transacts sales for a profit in his own store. Therefore, as a proprietor he is at liberty to treat customers in a somewhat authoritarian way. The professional role, on the other hand, demands an equalitarian approach to all clients. The professional dispenses expert services, not a product, and the services inhere in a structured, professional role. As a result the professional is constrained to treat all clients alike. Furthermore, professionals can perform the most personal of services for clients without any loss in status because their services *are* professional.

The professionals, like their fathers, desire racial harmony, and claim they learned how to get along with blacks when, as children, they worked in Chinese grocery stores. The males expressed satisfaction with the racial status quo. The females particularly the unmarried females, were not as contented, and some of them voiced a desire to become completely assimilated into white society. These women said assimilation was essential for social and economic equality. (They were probably right.) Most said they no longer had to fight the color line, although some female professionals still fear that the "colored" label has not completely disappeared and could be reenacted. Some indicated an affiliation with the wider community's power structure. For example, several male professionals told me that they were often privy to secret information about high-level business transactions and personal information about the ideas and actions of important townspeople. I probed on this point but received no further information. Perhaps they referred to investments and bank transactions.

One pharmacist talked about his position in the Delta:

> Being located here in the Delta is a natural for me. I come into contact with all social classes and all races of people. I respect them, and they respect me. As a professional I am invited to weddings and dinner parties hosted by white friends and associates. I feel no discrimination whatsoever. I am respectable, go to church, and work hard. Most other Chinese professionals are the same way. They will tell you that they are accepted too. I am confided in by a lot of important people.

My Delta experiences suggest that the professionals exaggerate their social and ethnic status. But again, my experience indicates that professionals in all ethnic groups have a similar tendency.

This group's prime identity is that of the professional. Its members declared that investments in and commitments to the professional role had provided them with extrinsic and intrinsic gratifications. They also talked about themselves as loving parents and husbands. Professionals call themselves Mississippians, Chinese Mississippians, Delta Mississippians, or Delta Chinese Mississippians. All of these self-designations denote a sense of place and an internalized personal identity. Some occasionally claim a Chinese cultural identity. Such identification appears symbolic rather than substantive. The professional's high aspirations, educational experiences, and necessary work contacts promote associations with whites and obviate sustained relations with blacks and some Chinese. The males say they are removed from businessmen's and old people's problems that relate to Chinese identity and preserving racial harmony. This statement accords with the fact that professionals of all groups lead somewhat exclusive lives, usually beyond the din and turmoil of everyday life. On the other hand, some female professionals, in contrast, are very much concerned with ethnic identity.

Professionals live in a wider, intellectually more stimulating environment than the marketplace world of their fathers. Their world requires a precise technical knowledge and approach rather than traditional and commonsense experience. They speak a different language (technical English) from their fathers' Delta vernacular and Cantonese. They also converse and associate with different kinds of people, mostly middle-class whites. The professional's world, then, is far removed from the Chinese grocery stores in black neighborhoods. Though this world is competitive, it is more secure and less vulnerable than that of the Chinese grocer. Professionals also live in a middle-class family atmosphere far removed from that of blacks and lower-class whites. The professional's social world at and away from home is affluent, secure, and pleasant.

Some professionals in a bantering fashion reported that some other professionals had become bananas, "yellow on the outside but white on the inside." This appellation would be derogatory if applied by outsiders. My observations suggest that most male professionals, though upwardly mobile like their white counterparts, are not ashamed of their Delta Chinese backgrounds. In fact they appear proud of their ethnicity. The professional's elevated social class seems to block out any negative ethnic feelings he might have about himself.

Professionals' View of Other Community Groups
Old People

Old people are the professional's grandfathers, relatives, and relatives' friends. Professionals described them as the Chinese pioneers in the Delta. They respect and love them, visit them, and invite them to their homes. They also listen to their stories and advice but avoid controversial subjects with them. Most professionals consider the old people too set in the Chinese way. One male chemist commented:

> The old people are well respected in the Delta. They first started the grocery stores and made their living working long hours every

day. But really their most important accomplishment was establishing the Chinese church and breaking us away from being categorized "colored." They established the Chinese as a separate individual group. I see this and many others do, too. We rarely talk about the past in my family, but my mother told me how bad it was for her and others to go to school. The old people fought for Chinese rights and prospered in the stores. They are courageous, thrifty, and sincere family people. Without them the younger generation could never have become professionals, but they are die-hard traditionalists. They stick to the old ways of thinking, but we respect them.

Some unmarried professional women consider them to be rigid, uncompromising, nosey, and dated in point of view.

Professionals know that old people view them as highly educated and successful members of the community. They also know that old people think that they have strayed too far from the Chinese way.

Businessmen

Businessmen are the professional's parents, relatives, and friends in the Chinese community. Professionals consider them to be successful, frugal, self-sacrificing merchants, family providers, and affectionate parents. They realize that the businessmen's economic and social success has passed down to them. Most still seek parental counsel. Professionals pointed out that their parents did not envy their affluent and American life-style —affluent, that is, as compared with that of the first two generations.

One male engineer declared:

We owe a large extent of our social and educational advancement to the businessmen. They taught us to survive in the Delta, sent us to college, and still act as guides and counselors. They always had it rough, working the stores and restaurants making sacrifices for us and prodding us to be different from them. I say without reservation that the businessmen bankrolled and put us in business. They seem to understand us and the problems we've faced, moving away from the old ways and into the modern ways. They helped us in being a bridge. Now it is up to the professional generation to do the same for their children.

Professionals know that businessmen recognize them as competent, intelligent, highly educated, successful children who have "made it" more than they themselves have.

College Students

Professionals described college students as their younger brothers, sisters, relatives, and friends who were similar to them in educational and occupational aspirations. They admire this group but think that some of them are being spoiled, that is, that some have too much money and free time to play. One accountant explained:

> The college students today have everything going for them. They have more time to go places and do things than our generation. We didn't have what they have. They seem to be more American-ized than my generation. But they'll do all right. They make good grades and will make good professional material. We look forward to their success when they graduate from school. They are just too spoiled now.

Professionals say that college students look up to them as professional role models, people who have opened up new ave-nues in society for them. They also think that the college stu-dent accepts their world view. The world views of male and female professionals vary, as we have seen.

Young People

Professionals defined members of this group as well-behaved and well-rounded children, nieces, nephews, and friends. They admire them for helping out in the grocery stores and restau-rants. Professionals said that young people were secure and confident because they had been brought up in economic pros-perity. One business manager remarked:

> Young people are bright, hard-working children who probably have the best chances in life. Their parents have economic secu-rity, and these young people prosper from it. The way I see it, these youngsters are level-headed, secure, and know what they want. They work hard at making good grades and friends. Young people are very disciplined, and I enjoy talking to them at ban-quets and other Chinese community events. They are winners.

Professionals think young people see them as important people who are more Caucasian than the old people or businessmen.

Women

Old women are grandmothers, mothers, and friends who have worked hard all their lives to build and maintain the Chinese community. Professionals also see them as traditional, demanding, and outdated first-generation Chinese. One nurse said: "The old women are really the creators and cornerstones of the Chinese community. They took care of the children, worked the store, and built the church. We admire, respect, and honor them for their self-sacrifices, intelligence, strong wills, and incredible foresight. They say what they wanted and worked to reach their goals. They wanted to be accepted as Chinese, and they got it. But they are out of date about a lot of things."

Professionals assume that old women recognize them as successful, educated, lucky people who have achieved prosperity and have brought pride to the Chinese community. They know that old people consider them too Americanized.

Professionals admire their young wives and young married female relatives and friends who are, like themselves, educated, modern, and independent.

As one teacher commented:

> The young married women have the opportunity of bringing up the next generation of Chinese. It will be a difficult task, but I am confident that they will manage and succeed. The new generation, of course, will be more Americanized than the previous one, but it will be stronger and fit in better with the present society. After all, we live in America, and so we will bring up our children in the American way.

Professionals think that young married women view them as successful, affluent, family men who are more equalitarian than first and second generation husbands.

Professionals identified young unmarried women as the most Americanized group in the Chinese community—much more Americanized than male counterparts. They said that unfortunately some of them placed career considerations before marriage. Some were seen as too outspoken and undisciplined. Male professionals stated that more of these women would become adjusted when they married. One engineer pointed out:

They are an independent lot, educated, outspoken, and goal oriented. The smart ones are aloof and have their ideas about marriage and a profession. They often take jobs away from the Delta so they can meet a man and get married. They don't seem to like to date the Chinese single men in the Delta. I guess it is because we all grew up together like one big family here, so that they are moving so far away from being Chinese that they are becoming like the whites. Most will marry Chinese and come around.

Unmarried female professionals said that many young unmarried women would eventually leave the Delta and become assimilated into white society. Professionals reported that these women pictured them as successful, highly educated Delta Chinese who were a little too traditional in value system and point of view. The single male professionals assumed that this group looked upon them as the most eligible bachelors in the Delta. I found this assumption to be correct.

The College Students

College students occupy the fourth position in the Mississippi Chinese community's deference hierarchy. Most of them are businessmen's children and range in age from the late teens to the mid-twenties. They were born in the middle class and, like the professionals, are pencil-and-paper oriented. Unlike professionals, their older brothers, sisters, and relatives, they speak little Cantonese, though they understand it fairly well. They speak Delta Southern English at home and in other settings, even when questions are put to them in Chinese by their parents and grandparents. When the elderly demand conversational exchange in Cantonese, they respond with pidgin Cantonese. College students see little utility in using Cantonese for communication among themselves or with others. They know generally about Chinese food, Chinese customs, and particularly about the grocery and restaurant businesses, as well as about race relations in the Delta. All have worked in Chinese businesses and have the native's understanding of the Delta cultural scene. All report that their parents placed pressure on them to excel at school and generally to succeed. Most have younger brothers and sisters in high school and older brothers and sisters in college or engaged in professional work. All have numerous relatives and friends in the Delta.

They drive late-model cars, which are usually high school graduation presents, and wear expensive casual clothes. Most own stereos and television sets. All appear middle class in tastes and outlook. Though most live on the campus, they return home frequently on weekends, holidays, and summer vacations to work in family businesses and to visit parents and relatives.

College Students at Home

Campus homes are usually at the University of Mississippi in Oxford, Mississippi State University in Starkville, and Delta State University in Cleveland. A few attend schools in Arkansas, Alabama, and Tennessee. Very few ever go to college farther away. When I asked them why, they answered with two basic reasons: "I don't want to go to school far away from my friends and family" and "My parents won't let me go to school far away."

College students live with relatives and other Chinese of the same sex in modest, middle-class houses and apartments. A few reside with whites. Those who live in dormitories, generally women, have similar companions. Parents prefer dormitory living arrangements for girls because dormitories offer a more sheltered environment. Student accommodations are comfortable but plain and reflect white students' tastes and styles. Chinese objects and symbols are conspicuously absent. Furniture consists of odd pieces such as those found in most college students' living quarters.

Students read, study, and party in their campus quarters. Chinese and white friends join them in eating, partying, watching television, and listening to music. They prefer black music —soul, blues, rhythm and blues, jazz—because, in their words, "it's the best music to listen and dance to." They dislike country and western music, which they call "redneck music." A similar view is found among blacks and some white students who favor jazz.

One student commented:

It feels so good to have my own place away from home. I can come and go as I please, have friends over, party, dance, and have a fun time without worrying my parents. It's a lot different here than at home in the Deltaland. I've made new friends and still keep the ones I met back home. I feel more freedom at school, and the world here seems broader.... there are more things to do at the university.

College Students at Work

The college students as a group perceive the academic setting to be a work setting. For example, one student declared: "When I'm at school, that's work to me." None reported any outside employment. All said their parents gave them enough money so they didn't have to work while attending school. They said jobs would take time away from their studies. Most were majoring in business, engineering, architecture, computer science, science, or math. None voiced any interest in future employment in state government or public service, and only a few were interested in the arts and humanities—where, they said, "there's no money." They see college as the way to a professional career.

The college students I talked to attend classes regularly, study hard, and apparently make good grades. Chinese students do not apply for scholarships, though some would qualify. They confide that scholarships, student politics, and campus organizations are dominated primarily by whites. None reported a nationalistic Chinese consciousness or an affiliation with overseas Chinese clubs on campus. They refer to overseas Chinese as "FOPs" ("fresh off the plane"). A few males participate in intramural sports at school because, they said, their parents had prevented them from participating in high school sports. One college student spoke about his academic focus in school, student activities, and work in the family business on weekends.

> I work hard in school to make high grades. I am quiet in the classroom most of the time, but I learn the material. I'm not a joiner of student organizations. Most of the other Chinese students aren't, either. We don't take part in that kind of stuff. It's hard to get into most organizations unless it's an honorary society. We just don't play the social scene because its dominated by whites. Before the Lucky Thirteen disbanded, we used to go to the dances. And some of my buddies and I play intramural basketball. Our parents wouldn't allow it when we were in high school because we had to study and work in the family business. It wasn't because we were Chinese, we just had to work. We sometimes work on weekends at the family business to help out and earn spending money. We don't plan to work in the business forever.

College Students at Church

College students are Christians of the Southern Baptist faith who have been "saved" and baptized. Most report active participation in church at school and at home, though they confided that religion had played a greater part in their lives earlier than at present. I observed that all attended church sporadically at school and regularly during home visits. This appears to be the case among most other college students in Mississippi. All members of the group I talked to appeared to be devout Christians. Like the professionals, most lacked knowledge of Chinese religions and deprecated Chinese religious practices in the Delta. One student's comments typified the group's religious attitudes and behavior.

> I and most of the college students I know are Christians, good ole Southern Baptist. That was part of growing up in the Delta, being looked upon by others as respectable and honest. Our parents used to make us go to church and Sunday school. But now most of us don't go too often unless we're at home. I still believe in God, Jesus Christ, and the whole thing, but now I see there are some interesting symbolic aspects to religion rather than the fire and brimstone we used to hear. For sure I don't believe in that Chinese supernatural stuff that some of the older generation gets into. I go to church with my parents, and I always will.

College Students at Leisure

College students spend leisure time, usually weekends and holidays, visiting with friends, family, and relatives. They say they appreciate the extended Chinese family more the longer they are at school. They visit their parents regularly, but their contacts with the old people are drastically reduced. This dearth of contacts with the elderly probably insulates them to a degree from a Chinese cultural identity and continuity. I noted in the interviews that college students live in the present and future and indicate little knowledge of (or interest in) either the historical mainland Chinese or the Delta Chinese past. In this respect they are quite different from the professionals, particularly the male professionals.

Students are vacationers, partygoers, and dancers. They take vacations in and out of Mississippi and visit relatives in California, Texas, Tennessee, and Georgia. Some of the more affluent go to Florida, Hawaii, and the Bahamas as tourists. The males are much more mobile in this respect than the females. They dance at discotheques, dine out, and go to parties hosted by friends. Very few are interested in college or professional athletic sports. They attend dances frequently held after Chinese wedding banquets, where they renew old acquaintances, chat, and socialize.

I stood one night on the periphery of the dance floor at one such event and conversed with a friend, two male college students, and three Chinese coeds. A seven-piece black band played rhythm-and-blues numbers. Champagne flowed, and everyone appeared to be having a good time. Dancing couples were a mixed group of young people, college students, and young professionals. A few businessmen and their wives and old people watched curiously, chatting at tables on the far side of the bandstand—away from the real action but near enough to see it. My observations told me much about the students' taste in music (they favor black music), their rejection of Chinese music, and their knowledge of the black American argot and demeanor.

One Chinese coed was enthusiastic. "The band's from Memphis and can really get it on." She moved in time with the music as if to emphasize her appreciation.

"What, no Chinese music for a Chinese wedding?" I asked.

"We don't like that singsongy music," said another coed. "And besides, you can't dance to it anyway."

"But the Chinese can dance to it. They do the gung fu."

"What's that?"

"Oh," I said casually, "that's a rather ancient dance step, way before your time." The coed broke off our conversation to dance, and I turned to a male college student. I extended my hand in a brotherly fashion and said, "Hey, brother . . ., what's happening?"

He returned the greeting in Afro-American argot: "You got da happening, brother." All of us laughed heartily, though I perceived that the women in the group were somewhat surprised and a little embarrassed by this exchange.[1]

Chinese roommates include "running buddies," "best friends," "good friends," and "cousins." These relationships among Chinese males involve much frequent, intensive and trusting social interaction.[2] The students attend parties, drink (moderately), and study together. College students rarely room with whites but regard a few as close friends. They report that off-campus social relationships are similar to those on campus.

Chinese female college students usually room with other Chinese coeds, their sisters, cousins, relatives, and friends. Friendship ties, networks, and work activities are similar to those of Chinese males. Some more independent Chinese coeds report white coed roommates. Coeds say their brothers often attend the same school and exert some supervision over their social relations.

College students relate that socializing occurs in twosomes or groups based on friendship, social class, and family-clan networks. Students go to parties, dinners, and the movies in mixed uncoupled sex groups. Some friends are members of families whom they had previously known in the Chinese community, while others are new friends.

[1]The Chinese college students at no time indicated to me that they possessed more than a superficial knowledge of black culture. For the most part, their presentation of self fits the norms of the Southern white culture with which they feel most comfortable, and although black and white cultures have mixed to some extent, the students express little awareness of the fact.

[2]These Chinese sociometric network categories were similar in form and substance to those discovered by Liebow in his study of Negro streetcorner men. The closest primary friendships center around the individual with whom each man interacts on a daily basis and with whom he exchanges emergency aid, comfort, or support in crises or in other times of need. Chinese college students refer to such friendship relations as "family." Acquaintances lie on the periphery of the individual's sociometric network and are referred to as people whose identity is "known about." Chinese report that such acquaintance relationships are secondary, not face-to-face, contacts on a daily basis and lack depth. Chinese males rarely have white male friends as fictive kinsmen or "brothers." Close white male companions are referred to as "friends" or "close friends," without the adjectives "good" or "best." For an interesting discussion of Liebow's findings regarding black friendship configurations, see Elliot Liebow, *Tally's Corner* (Boston: Little, Brown, 1967), pp. 161–207, especially pp. 162–166. An excellent treatment of the degree of reciprocal knowledge in the social relationships of acquaintance and friendship may be found in Kurt H. Wolff, *The Sociology of Georg Simmel* (New York: Free Press, 1950), pp. 320–326.

Chinese parents demand that college students refrain from dating while in school so that they can concentrate on studying. Students state (and my observations confirm) frequent violations of parental wishes in this area. Chinese parents reluctantly accept dating relationships among Chinese students but insist that dating couples postpone marriage until after graduation. Males infrequently date Chinese coeds or maintain "steady" relationships with them. Instead, they either "hang out with the boys" or go out in friendly heterosexual mixed racial groups. Some few males date white coeds surreptitiously. They said that "white girls like to go out and have fun, are easier to talk to, and are more interesting than Chinese girls, who are stuck up, sheltered, spoiled, and don't know what's happening."[3] Very few Chinese students were tagged "playboys" by peers. Most males did not date.

Chinese coeds disclose an ambivalent attitude toward Chinese college males. They like to date other Chinese occasionally but find them to be quiet, socially immature, shy, inhibited boys who do not ask them out. The reciprocated pseudonegative image does not foster congenial dating and mating. Chinese coeds pretend to take an insouciant attitude toward Chinese males who date white coeds. They underscore that Chinese male students have more freedom than they themselves do in the dating area. One coed said:

> The Chinese boys have more freedom than the girls. They can go as they please as long as they don't get into big trouble. If they date a white girl, they usually are discrete about it. If the word gets out because they weren't cool or somebody didn't keep their mouth shut, then their reputation is hurt in the Chinese community. It shouldn't be that way for any of us, but that's "show biz," honey! And we have to live with it. Most of the Chinese men don't get too serious with white girls, and most don't marry them. And

[3]Many men (from different ethnic groups) refer to females of another ethnicity as more exotic, daring, or charming than the "good women" in their particular group. And some prefer to socialize outside their own group. Some ethnic females feel freer with males from groups other than their own. Like may attract like, but for some the exotic outsider is appealing, especially for romantic and/or sexual interludes. Group taboos against interracial or ethnic intimate relations sometimes whet sexual appetites. In this particular case the Chinese boys may have been bragging; they may have also been giving an excuse for not asking Chinese girls when the real reason was simply shyness.

most white girls, don't get serious with Chinese boys. If they catch us dating white boys it's worse.

Chinese coeds confide that the possibilities of finding a mate are rare because the Chinese male is shy and because many of the students from the Delta are interrelated. They also insist that it is hard to remain a "good girl" and retain an unblemished reputation in the Chinese community. For example, they claim that any serious negative rumor about their virginity could easily ruin their chances of finding a mate. One coed talked about this problem:

> If you haven't found out already, the gossip network here in the Delta is pernicious. I mean if anyone sneezes, everybody and their mother gets the wind of it. I personally don't care what people want to do. That's their business. But you know how people with small minds are . . ., they like to get vicious, especially if they're jealous or envious or something. They will fabricate lies or exaggerate something and put it on someone they don't like. For example, if someone's single and another doesn't like her, they might say that she takes the pill and runs around. You see, automatically that person is labeled promiscuous. Or they could drum up some story that a Chinese girl is running around with white guys. That would ruin her standing in the community and darken her possibilities for marriage because she's been "had," used merchandise. She would catch hell by her family, and protesting the rumor would only make the situation worse than it was before. She could lose face and be socially disgraced.[4]

Coeds state that parents and Chinese males oppose interracial dating. Parents fear that their daughters might lose their reputations and their virginity. Chinese coeds and males become jealous. Coeds who spoke to me claimed that they either sneaked out with whites or waited for the reluctant Chinese males to ask them out. Only a few Chinese girls reported going out with white college men regularly. The attitudes that Chinese males expressed to me about Chinese females who dated whites were contradictory. They said on the one hand "It

[4]Clearly this is an example of the process of informal labeling discussed by Becker. The social rules in the Chinese community define chastity and endogamy as right actions (being a "good girl") and those who engage in misconduct (promiscuity) are seen as outsiders who cannot be trusted to live by the rules agreed upon by the group. See Howard S. Becker, *Outsiders: Studies in the Sociology of Deviance* (New York: Free Press, 1963), p. 1.

is disgusting," while on the other hand (tacitly approving), they said, "It's not my business to tell them what to do, but if they want to date the whites, it's okay."

Chinese coeds submit that intimate heterosexual relationships are rare in college. This statement is probably true. It was my observation, however, that the pressure to remain a "good girl" is difficult for women to cope with. To avoid an unbesmirched image the coed must seem gregarious (not unlike the upper-middle-class Southern belle, she must have a seductive, friendly, sexy, coquettish, glamorous, and self-contained poise that is also virginal, fastidious, and ladylike). This behavior permits her to be at least approachable and acceptable but also to remain a lady.[5]

The changing sexual mores of this generation pose problems for students in the areas of courtship and marriage. Most would prefer an endogamous marriage. Still, it is generally easier for Chinese coeds to date whites than to date Chinese males. Intermarriages, when they do occur, usually involve white males and Chinese females. Whatever the Chinese male's dating situation, he remains true to Chinese tradition: "They eventually marry a Chinese woman when the time has come." Male and female students are much more open-minded about interracial dating and marrying with whites than the professionals are.

College Students in the Triethnic Community

College students say they are not asked to join social fraternities and sororities at the larger universities. This discrimination, they feel, blocks their complete acceptance and assimilation into the white Southern social system. College students contend that if one is Chinese, wealth and strong political connections are required for membership in fraternities or sororities. One student remarked:

The whites run the fraternities and sororities and decide who they want to let in and who they want to keep out. I know a few of my Chinese friends have tried to get in, but to no avail. You might

[5]For a more elaborate discussion of Southern coquetry, see Florence King, *Southern Ladies and Gentlemen* (New York: Stein and Day, 1975).

make it at open rush, but when it comes to formal rush, you don't receive the bids. It takes money to buy expensive wardrobes and contacts with the right kinds of people in the right places, like the governor and lineage. Well, we don't have white lineage. It is very difficult to overcome the race barrier, not just the social one.

Another college student spoke further about the line that separates Chinese from whites on the college campus.

The whites will accept you at every level, but not socially. Whites are still concerned with the social line, like the DAR [Daughters of the American Revolution]. At Ole Miss it's real tough to get in, and you might as well forget it. I know of a Chinese boy who was accepted into a high-class fraternity at State, but his father's got connections. His father is an alumnus, and he contributes $10,000 a year to the university. With that kind of money I'd buy me a Lear Jet and fly above all that social bulljive and . . .

College students occasionally talked about their high school experiences and particularly about school segregation in the Delta, which, they contended, was based on social class as well as race. Those Chinese who lived in white neighborhoods went to white schools automatically. The students claimed, however, that most Chinese lived in the black neighborhoods or working-class white neighborhoods where most school integration took place. Students recalled the strategies the Chinese had used to avoid sending their children to school with blacks. The children either stayed with relatives who lived in white neighborhoods or used addresses of fictitious relatives in white neighborhoods. A few Chinese students attended private academies. Some who lived behind the stores in the black neighborhood reluctantly attended black schools because their parents feared the loss of black customers should they attend private schools. One college student commented on the school problem:

When the Chinese say that they have come a long ways, they mean it seriously. The town that I live in is mapped out and zoned in such a way as to segregate the blacks from the whites. I wasn't as lucky as those Chinese who lived in the middle-class white neighborhoods because they went to the white high school. And I didn't go to a private academy. We lived across town, and it was zoned for blacks. I refused to go there because their teachers and equipment were inferior to white schools. Besides, we ran a store, and I came into contact with them all the time. Frankly, I don't feel right going to school with them. So I told the school authorities that I lived over in the middle-class white neighborhood because my uncle's last name and mine are identical. I got in and did that for four years.

Another college student talked about the problems of attending black schools.

I was lucky, but there was a Chinese girl who had to go to the black high school because her parents lived behind the store in the black neighborhood. She came out of there talking and acting just like one of them. It couldn't be helped, and I feel sorry for her. Her parents were afraid if she didn't go there, the blacks would stop buying groceries from them, or even worse, burn down their store to spite them. I can't blame them for doing what was necessary to survive.[6]

College students, like the professionals, are upwardly mobile like their white counterparts: they desire to attend white schools, join white social organizations, enter the professions, and date whites occasionally. Many whites are not interested in encouraging Chinese to do so. In fact, some whites have blocked this aspiration to some extent. Actually, college students manifest cultural traits of all three groups in the triethnic society: (1) Delta Chinese—some filial piety, traditional diet and customs; (2) Delta white—the Southern Baptist religious orientation, language, speech patterns, aspirations, customs, racial etiquette; (3) Delta black—music, argot, some speech patterns, the dance, and some body language. Most white Southerners possess elements of (2) and (3).

Students think of themselves as students, Mississippians, Americans, and Delta Chinese. They aspire to professional status and a professional identity in or outside the Delta. Some, particularly males, would prefer to remain in Mississippi or at least in the South. Most would prefer to leave the Delta. All are unmistakably Southerners, though they are still struggling with an ethnic identity problem. They are neither white nor Chinese. One would expect to find such a problem among most

[6]The problem here was probably the quality of the school rather than racial composition. But the reports concentrated on racial differences rather than on cultural differences, an error made by many ethnic groups when judging other ethnic groups.

ethnic college students. For the Chinese students, the solution remains a question. Some appear to be more traditional than others, although most are much more assimilated than other community groups. Others especially some females, seem to prefer a white identity. All are middle class in orientation.

The group's world view, though somewhat amorphous, centers on a college environment and a student's role. Their world consists of social and academic rounds of college life and the people and objects it encompasses. Unlike their role models, the professionals, the college students have no clearly defined identity or world view.[7] As Delta Chinese they are struggling in a white world in which they desire upward mobility. They expressed some anxieties associated with the quest for social acceptance in the local and wider community as Mississippians and Americans.

Many have attempted to adopt the Southern white's self-concept, world view, and life-style but have been rebuffed and have been told that they are not quite white enough. A Chinese world is impossible. The Delta Chinese world appears too narrow and confining to many. They do not desire to be classified with blacks. As a result they straddle two cultural worlds, those of Delta Chinese and of Delta white America. One Chinese male student talked about his identity and world view.

> I once thought that I knew exactly who I was, but I don't any more. I'm unsure and confused. In high school I saw myself at first as Delta Chinese, but my friends and everyone treated me as a white American. Then, when I went to college, I tried to be in with the whites, and they told me I was Chinese and sort of shunned me. I feel it, and it hurts. I guess, then, that I am both Chinese and American, but I don't feel comfortable being Chinese, and I cannot be white. It seems like I don't belong in either world. I just think of myself as a person: it's safer that way. All of us are brothers under the skin in this world. I hope I will eventually get out of this confusion. Maybe when I get my degree in pharmacy it'll be different.... I'll be somebody then. But one thing is for sure, we ain't "colored" any more.

[7]College students, unlike professionals, willingly discussed their mixed feelings about themselves and society with me. Professionals, now successful, refused to dwell on past prejudice and discrimination.

Most would like to immerse themselves in a white professional world.

College Students' View of Other Community Groups
Old People

Old people are their grandparents, relatives, and relatives' friends. The students regard the elderly as traditional, old-fashioned, critical, and respectable community members. One male student spoke about the first generation:

> The old people are the Chinese pioneers in the Delta. They had it rough. But they worked hard and created a place for themselves and for us. We love them, but they're kind of old-fashioned and critical when it comes to the new generation. They think their old ways are best. The times have just changed faster than what they're willing to accept. They want us to speak Cantonese to them. I do the best I can, but who has time for that stuff?

Though all female students expressed love and respect for their grandparents, some resented those who (they said) interfered in their personal lives, particularly in the areas of dress, personal freedom, career plans, travel, living arrangements, and dating. College students think old people see them as industrious, intelligent, respectful, independent, and confused young people who are slipping away from the traditional Chinese ways.

Businessmen

College students perceive businessmen as their fathers, uncles, relatives, friends, counselors, and leaders in the Chinese community. They are also seen as successful, enterprising merchants who serve as a cultural bridge to the past because their behavior and ideas form a wholesome mixture of the old Chinese ways and the new American ways. Students described businessmen as less rigid and more understanding than grandparents. A college student characterized businessmen: "The Chinese businessmen are sharp, hard-working merchants who know how to make and save money. They are successful and wise. They understand the college generation because they have a Chinese and American background. They're very supportive in school. They are conservative people who avoid trouble, go to church, and head the family. They are generous and pay for our education." Some college females see businessmen as too strict and protective. College students think businessmen see them as ambitious, independent, respectful, fun-loving children who are rapidly becoming westernized.

Professionals

Professionals are successful brothers, sisters, relatives, and friends who have finished school and found good positions. Students recognize their similarity to the professionals, their role models. Most said professionals were easy and pleasant to talk to because the professionals understood students. One male student commented:

> The professionals have it made, being successful and independent. They no longer have to answer to anyone. What they do is their own business. They are respected by everyone. We see them as heroes, and we want to be like them. They know who they are and don't seem to have many worries. They make good money and live a carefree life. We hope that they will open some doors for us when we graduate. It's so nice to see people who are happy.

Most female college students view male professionals as potential mates as well as career models. Many coeds perceive male professionals at the same time as too traditional and passive. Still other coeds, who plan to leave the Delta after graduation, do not consider professionals eligible mates. Members of the latter group say they will marry on the basis of individual reasons rather than because of race or ethnicity and definitely do not plan to marry Delta males. College students think professionals see them as a group of young students similar in viewpoint and assets to themselves and likely soon to join them in the professional ranks. They know that professionals recognize and empathize with their life situation and identity conflicts.

Young People

Young people are brothers, sisters, nieces, nephews, cousins, and friends, who are secure and happy at home. This group will soon join the students at college. Students see them as sheltered, inexperienced "model children." They report that the professional's children are more Americanized than the children of other community groups. One college student commented on the situation of young people and suggested that they must eventually leave the Delta in order to succeed.

> These kids are very intelligent and have much going for them, especially the children of professionals. They are brought up in more Americanized homes. Of course, all Chinese parents push their children to succeed, but the professional's children will have a better chance at life, especially those who live in the city and go to preschool and good elementary schools and high schools. Those children have it better than we did in the Delta. But children do okay in the Delta in spite of the rednecks. If you don't believe me, just look around downtown, and you'll see what I mean. If the Chinese are ever going to really make it big in the world, they will have to leave the Delta. It's that simple.

Some students feel these young people are too sheltered and too spoiled at home. Female students appear to identify with them more than males do. College students think younger brothers and sisters see them as hard-working, fun-loving, independent, lucky people who are removed from the family environment and are going to school with the aim of becoming professionals.

Women

Old women are respected grandmothers, relatives, and relatives' friends. They attempt to maintain the Chinese identity and culture and to practice Chinese customs. They also manage festivities during the Chinese New Year and the Harvest Moon. Old women always know what to do when people are married, become sick, or die. On the other hand, some students said many of these women are old-fashioned, rigid, and dogmatic— and sometimes mean when they try to rule the younger generation. Coeds appear to be more in conflict with grandmothers than male students, especially those coeds who wish to date (and do date) whites. One coed criticized old women.

> The old women can become extremely reactionary when it concerns marriage outside of the Chinese way. I remember one time this couple wanted to get married and they had the same last name. The old women raised hell and said that that kind of Chi-

nese incest would not be proper and would bring bad luck to the couple as well as their families. The couple got married anyway, and the conflict blew over after a while. In another case, I heard about one old woman who raised hell about a Chinese girl marrying a white guy. They were so outraged, they performed a funeral for her to let her know she was no longer a living member of her family. That incident was really cruel, but that was how the old women felt about Chinese-white marriages. That event shook a lot of people up and scared many Chinese girls who had any ideas of trying to do it in the Delta. I mean those old fogies not only shunned her, they ostracized her from the Chinese community and family. That's how extreme they can get![8]

Often coeds criticize grandmothers in general or somebody else's grandmother rather than their own. This tendency probably permits the coeds to express love and respect for their grandmothers while still discharging resentment. College students think old women view them as modern, Americanized young people who are slipping away from the Chinese ways. However, they think that old women know they will succeed as professionals and bring honor, pride, and respect to themselves, their families, and the Chinese community. Some coeds think that old women are too critical of them.

Young married women—sisters, relatives, and friends—are educated, modern, successful females and good wives and mothers, frequently employed as professionals. One male college student remarked: "The young married women have done well. They are educated and smart. They married young Chinese professionals and are very successful. Their children are bright and will become successful, too. We get along with them because they are so modern in their outlook on life. They think a lot like we think." Some coeds think their older married sisters are too compliant and conservative. College students think young married women see them as struggling, intelligent students who will eventually follow in their footsteps; having earned their degrees, the students will marry Chinese mates and will remain close to their families.

[8]I question whether such a ceremony was actually performed. The story was probably constructed as a scare tactic or simply to reaffirm ethnic identity. Similar ceremonies, reported by many ethnic groups, have not been confirmed.

Young unmarried women are single college graduates, sisters, relatives, and friends. Students describe them as independent, educated, career oriented, outspoken, socially mature females. They say these women are currently seeking mates and/or professional careers. Students state that these women are the most Americanized group in the Chinese community. The male students see many of them as strong, superior, "stuck-up" women who may have some difficulty in finding husbands. Some students find these women overbearing. One male student reported:

> The single girls who have graduated from college move more quickly into the American scene than boys. They are educated, independent and looking for marriage to someone who is equally intelligent and career minded. Most of them will probably have to leave the Delta to find what they want. There aren't too many men of that description around. They are going to be very successful. Some are kind of aloof and flip, but they are easy to talk to once you get to know them. Sometimes it takes a lot of time. They put some guys down without trying. You got to be on the ball for them.

Many college coeds identify with these women and view them as an emotionally mature, independent, modern, successful group. Some coeds say of their own group that some will never marry men from the Delta. As one coed reported, such college students "will be moving on."

The Young People

Young people hold the fifth position in the Mississippi Chinese community's deference hierarchy. The children (and some grandchildren) of businessmen and professionals, they range in age from infancy through high school —those years when they are under the aegis of parents. The older young people of high school age, businessmen's children, attend public and private junior high and high schools in the Delta. Most of the younger children, professionals' children, are enrolled in private academy schools. Products of the middle to upper-middle class, all are sensitized to Delta Chinese culture by their grandmothers, parents, aunts, and uncles in the Chinese community. Businessmen's children demonstrate more verbal ability in Cantonese than do professionals' children. A few professional families have elderly relatives living with them who attempt to teach the children some Cantonese and some appreciation of Chinese customs. A few of the youngsters more fluent in Chinese are the children of Hong Kong refugees who immigrated during the 1960s. All young people speak English in all behavior settings. They are similar to college students in many ways, and their speech patterns, inflection, and style of diction reflect the Southern Delta vernacular. Most appear strong and healthy, and most present a self-assured manner in the presence of others.

Young People at Home

Young people report that their standing in the community is based on their father's status. They know in a general way that status depends on wealth, residence, size of business, and education. They are well-disciplined, well-behaved, noncompetitive, secure children at home, where they respect parental authority within the Chinese familial hierarchy. Children never call parents by their first names, and they address elders according to an age hierarchy. For example, they call the oldest brother, *Ah Goo* ("number one"), and the eldest sister, *Ah Dee*. They address younger siblings by numerical order, that is "number two," "number three," and so forth. The older children claim to share among themselves the labor of supervising the younger ones, but the mother always takes care of the infant in the family.[1]

Because the maintenance of the family unit takes precedence over individual needs, everything is shared. Sibling rivalry is viewed as shameful behavior, and the older children are usually instructed to sacrifice individual pleasures for young children. Family solidarity and maintenance follows the Confucian values of mutual sharing, filial piety, and deference to elders. Young people try to control (as they are taught) expressions of emotion (for example, excitement, sadness, and aggression) in their interactions with one another and with parents. They do not talk back to parents and never shout to anyone. Youngsters learn about competition from their parents and from personal observations (at business and at school), but they do not compete at home.

Parents negotiate disagreements away from the children. Parents seldom display affection toward each when children are present. The family does provide frequent, intense primary group interactions as well as connecting links between children and the community. Young people attribute much of their security to the knowledge that their parents love each other and their offspring. Love is never made contingent on fulfillment of some obligation. Parents always extend love, though they may express disapproval of their children's misconduct.

One young person of elementary school age talked about

---

[1]The association between Delta Chinese children and their parents differs from that found in white Delta families. For example, Chinese families rarely if ever place the child under the supervision of outsiders. Baby-sitters are never used, because family members are always available.

family devotion, respect for elders, and the relationship of parents to children at home.

> There are four children in our home, and I am the middle child. I have an older brother who is going to junior high, a younger sister in fourth grade, and a baby brother two years old. My daddy runs a grocery store in town, and all of us stay there in the back of the store. We live in the back. My daddy gives us all chores to do, but he says that our studies are the most important. We all help each other like in a club. Daddy is the president, Mommy is the vice president, and my older brother is the sergeant at arms. Mommy and Daddy are happy about all of us and love us very much. I think that I am daddy's favorite. He hugs me a lot more than he does mommy.

Young People at Work

The familial play and work worlds of *Ching Nen* are inextricably intertwined and provide them with an integrated, stable, and consistent environment. At their parent's business they study, play, eat, sweep the floor, stack merchandise, prepare food, and wait on customers. Older children of high school age are given greater work responsibility than younger children. For example, they operate the cash register, make change, help customers, and assemble take-out orders. These older children demonstrate sharp, calculating minds and methodical procedures in handling money and managing customers. All are skillful in the art of salesmanship with blacks and whites. Their behavior behind the counter differs from that of white boys of the same age in white stores, who do not take work as seriously, show less ability to make a sale, and make more mistakes in counting change. Young people are awarded a small "allowance" to spend on movies or hobbies.[2] Chinese young people associate more frequently with adults outside the family unit than do most white children. They told me that early experience with "outside" adults helped them develop an awareness

[2]Chinese children are not necessarily given an allowance for work they do for their parents. They do receive spending money for entertainment, however. The value of work is not considered an individualized effort: all work together as a family unit, earning and spending money. Thus work is linked to family economic solidarity, and money is only considered a means, not an end in itself.

Young people help out at the family store by running the "front" and operating the cash register, stacking groceries, running errands, etc. Early experience with "outside" adults helps them to develop an awareness of correct behavior in the Delta.

of correct behavior in the Delta, for example, proper race relations. All said they become aware early of family budgets and of the need to save for school expenses and other expenditures such as dental work and orthodontic and eye care.

In the work setting young people study and do homework during slack periods. They aspire to a college education and a higher social and economic status than that of their parents. One teenager described the life-style and attitudes of the young in the work setting:

My father has a restaurant, and I usually go there after school to help out during the rush hour around five-thirty. I would like to play high school sports, but the family business comes first. I help fry prawns, run errands for the cooks, and help the dishwasher. Around eight to eight-thirty the dinner rush is over, so I go home and study. In a couple of years, I plan to go to college like most of my friends. My parents have always drilled in me the value of education and professional success. They don't want me to end up cooking over a stove every day . . ., and they're right.

Young children of the increasing professional class do not work. They spend free time playing with friends, participating in extracurricular school activities, visiting relatives, watching television, reading, and taking part in church programs. Some children take dancing and music lessons. One professional's daughter of junior high school age talked to me about her school activities:

My daddy is an accountant and my momma works as a part-time pharmacist. There are only three children in the family. I am in the middle. I like junior high school very much. I play flute in the band. I play volleyball after school. I am secretary of the student council and take ballet lessons. I'm a good student, and everyone likes me at school. I have a lot of friends, but my mother won't let me date yet because I'm too young. But many boys at school think I'm cute. They talk to me at lunch all the time.

This excerpt vividly suggests the young girl's middle-class status and life-style.

Young People at Church

Most young people are members of the Southern Baptist church and attend Sunday school and church services regularly. All read the Bible and relate Bible stories; all know Southern Baptist theology. They participate in church activities (for example, the Baptist Youth Union, choir, and church socials). One young person expressed this group's religious attitudes and behavior:

I'm a Christian, and I was saved about a year ago. . . . that's when I was eleven years old. It was a very important experience for me because all of my friends and parents were pulling for me. I go to Sunday school and sing in the youth choir. It's a lot of fun, and

I enjoy being with my friends at church. All the people at our church are very nice and respected people. We all feel a close relationship with each other when we worship God.

Young people are expected to be "saved" and to be committed to Jesus Christ and are baptized between the ages of ten or eleven and fifteen to twenty. Most are baptized before they are fifteen. The public commitment to Christ in church provides a time of joy and reverence for both the individual and the congregation. One is taught what it means to be saved early on, and therefore this religious experience is viewed as a "natural" event. Baptism completes the process of being saved; one then has been born again. The emphasis here is on the correct belief system rather than on good deeds. Much of the Chinese community's social life for all age groups revolves around the church.

Young People at Leisure

Most leisure activity takes place around the home and work settings with brothers and sisters, relatives, and others who live nearby. young people claim they rarely play with blacks or whites.[3] Junior and senior high school students attend parties in parent's homes, where males interact on a cross-sex and group basis. They do not date. Young people read books, work crossword puzzles, collect stamps and insects, construct models, skip rope, and play ball, tag, hopscotch. In short, their leisure activities are similar in many respects to those of middle-class white children, though they are more home centered and parent supervised.

One young person remarked on parental supervision:

My momma always kept an eye on us and made sure we behaved. When she used to smoke, she would never smoke around us kids. She'd always hide out in the bathroom. She gave it up after a while, and she told us not to ever smoke. If we were going to see

[3] I question whether Chinese children did not play with blacks, because many grew up in the black neighborhoods in and around the Chinese grocery stores. All of the individuals I interviewed insisted that they did not play with blacks. If they did not, it was probably because they found playmates within their own large families.

a friend, she'd always drive us over and tell us not to stay late or end up eating supper there. She'd always tell us to call her to let her know where we were. When we got older she would lecture to us about cutting school, marijuana, drinking, and all that stuff. She told us that if she ever heard that we did any of that stuff, she'd whip us until we couldn't walk and then send us to French Camp to juvenile prison. So we never got into trouble like some of the blacks and whites did at school.

Young people travel out of state with the family on vacations and receive visits from relatives who live outside Mississippi. These contacts place the children in touch with some of the world beyond the Delta and the Mississippi River. One youngster told me about some visitors from the outside:

> Last summer my cousins from Los Angeles came to visit us. They are in junior high like I am. Their daddy runs a grocery store, too. We spent a lot of time chewing the fat because we don't write too much to each other. We took them to see *Smokey and the Bandit*, about these guys who have CB [citizens' band] radios carrying a truck load of beer across the country chased by a county sheriff. I thought the show was real cool, but my cousins didn't think so. I guess they like the big city better than the country. They like to go to museums, to the beach, and amusement parks. We don't have that around here. I'd like to go and live in California some day. When I get there I might like it and stay. It sure beats staying around the Delta, 'cause there's nothing to do here for excitement. All anyone does is cruise town, and there ain't much of town, or go riding in the country, and that's most everywhere.

Apparently the grass elsewhere appears greener to these children; on the other hand, a visit is not a permanent move. Some Delta youngsters told me they were glad to get back home after returning from long visits out of the state.

Young People in the Triethnic Community

Young people claim to be accepted by both blacks and whites and to get along with both groups. Parents have taught them the "proper" etiquette of race relations, and though they show no overt hostility toward blacks or whites, they prefer white models to blacks. They know the surface problems of race relations in the Delta but do not understand the ideology of class and race that underlies the situation. These youngsters conduct themselves in a formal, polite manner and address white adults as "sir" and "mam" as in customary in the South. Like college students, they express a preference for black music and show a familiarity with the black argot.

They report a desire for acceptance and integration into the Delta white society but claim to have difficulty in attending predominantly white schools. Most do not live in middle-class white neighborhoods. The earlier practice of establishing residence in white neighborhoods (by assuming fictitious addresses) has been successfully challenged and defeated at an accelerating rate during the past five years.[4] Consequently some businessmen have moved to middle-class white residential areas. Young people say that discrimination against the Chinese in real estate practices has eased, so that some Chinese families have been able to move into middle-class white neighborhoods. Some businessmen have bought mobile homes and have placed them in white residential areas to establish legal residence for their children. The mobile homes usually house two or more Delta Chinese students. Some attend white private schools in the Delta.

One private school student commented on the high costs involved, tensions with white residency, and the desire to attend white schools in order to escape from the blacks:

> The private school offers the best instruction, equipment, and supervision but is the costliest. My parents didn't want the hassle that other Chinese parents were going through trying to establish white residency, so they enrolled me and my brother in private school after the sixth grade. They wanted us to go to white schools. They had to pay $200 to get us in. Then my father becomes a stockholder. Each year he has to pay $1,000 for my brother and me. My mother has to give us rides to and from school each day. We also have to buy our own books because the state government doesn't supplement the school. It costs about as much to go to the academy as it does to go to college. Our parents really have to save

[4]Whites appear to be much less concerned about the mixing of Chinese and black schoolchildren than are the Chinese. The burden of maintaining identity as a third group still rests heavily on the Chinese. One wonders how the blacks feel about racial mixture with the Chinese. Fragmentary reports suggest that they have no strong feelings one way or the other. Middle-class blacks in urban areas frequently enroll their children in Catholic parochial schools, which they feel provide a better education than public schools.

money for us to go to school. I know it is hard on them because they are always buying things for us, but never for themselves. But we don't really want to go to school with blacks.

Young people profess some Chinese ethnic consciousness, as I learned one afternoon during a conversation with two brothers. The topic was a martial arts film, Bruce Lee's *Enter the Dragon,* which was currently showing nearby. One of Lee's weapons in the film is a set of nunchuks, two hardwood sticks twelve inches long connected at one end by a length of chain.[5] The boys, ten and thirteen years old, expressed enthusiastic admiration of Lee's skill with nunchuks. With a little encouragement from me, they brought out their own pair, and after I had shown them the pair I owned strung with parachute cord, the three of us took turns demonstrating nunchuk techniques. For these boys and others whom I met, Bruce Lee synthesized Chinese and American values in an appealing philosophy of individualism, independence, self-discipline, and hard work.

Young people claim a number of identities that are in flux, as one would expect, given the range in ages and the process of growth. Young people see themselves at home as the fortunate children of businessmen and professionals. At work they are "helpers" who assist in the family business. They define themselves as good, hard-working students at school. They are Southern Baptists at church and in the community. Adolescents refer to themselves as Delta Chinese. Young people appear to have no identity problems until they reach college age. Though males and females are Americanized by the late teens, girls appear to assimilate more rapidly than boys.[6]

[5]Nunchuks, or nunchakus, were originally made from hardwood and were strung together by rope braided from horses' tails. Rice farmers first used them for thrashing rice. Later they came into use as a weapon of self-defense. See Fumio Demura, *Nunchaku: Karate Weapon of Self Defense* (Burbank, Calif.: Ohara Publications, 1971). Bruce Lee was a Chinese-American film star and cultural hero born in San Francisco and reared in Hong Kong who died in 1973 at the age of thirty-three.

[6]This observation concerning assimilation rates of boys and girls is impressionistic. It may be, however, that boys assimilate more slowly than girls because the Chinese patriarchal system expects boys to remain more closely allied with the Chinese ways in order to fulfill their filial duties. Following Chinese patriarchal belief, a male upon marriage adds to his family, whereas a female becomes an extension of her husband's family (and moves away from home). Thus marital

Young people do not have a solidified world view. Preadolescents see the world in terms of family, school, and church; their world is a restricted, pleasant, secure, and sheltered taken-for-granted place. Adolescents' world view seems to range somewhere between that of businessmen and college students. They, too, talk about the world as a competitive arena where the good, educated, frugal, intelligent, and hard-working people succeed and the rest fail. There appears to be little if any concern with what happens to those who fail. They visualize a future world similar to that of the professionals, and frequently this hoped-for world is beyong the Delta and Mississippi. One high school senior talked about his outlook on college, a career outside Mississippi, and his parent's growing acceptance of outmigration.

> Next year I'll be going to State to take up electrical engineering. I hope that after I graduate from college the job market will be good. My brother is also in EE and working in Houston. I hope to go and join him there. Maybe he can get me into the same company he works for. Right now he's very successful and has found a girl that he likes. I hope to follow in his footsteps. There's nothing to keep me in the Delta—it's too small of a world, and it lacks opportunities. My parents are beginning to understand that.

Everyone will not attain professional status, and one wonders what will become of those who do not.

Young People's View of Other Community Groups
Old People

Old people are grandparents, relatives, and relatives' friends. The young love and respect this group. The preadolescents seem to enjoy closer ties with them than the older youngsters do. One adolescent remarked of the old people's legacy:

> My father tells me that my grandpa used to run and own a small grocery store while he was still alive. He contributed money to

---

expectations and familial exclusion for the Chinese female, along with the females' generally faster r 'e of maturation, may serve to accelerate assimilation. It was further observed that Chinese patriarchs visited the families of sons more frequently than those of daughters. Family business matters are more frequently handled by sons than by sons-in-law.

build the Mission school and sent my father there. My father later gave money to help build the Chinese church. Those old people were the pioneers of the Chinese community. They have passed down the Chinese customs and made us Chinese. We are not old-fashioned like they are. But I have a deep respect for their ways. Every time I go to the Chinese Church I look across the lot to the Mission School, it's old and run down, but during its heydey it must have been jumping. Sometimes if I imagine real hard I can hear Chinese kids playing and talking in the schoolyard, their voices echoing off the walls of the building.

Young people think old people see them as growing up to become educated and successful. They think the elderly hope to live long enough to see them graduate from high school and go on to college.

Businessmen

Young people see businessmen as fathers, uncles, relatives, and relatives' friends who operate successful grocery stores and restaurants in the Delta. Businessmen serve as cultural bridges between the old Chinese and the new American ways. The young do not consider the businessmen as old-fashioned as old people are, that is, the businessmen seem to have been able to change with the times. One young person characterized businessmen:

> The businessmen are in touch with what goes on today as well as the old Chinese customs. I can relate to them because they have a lot of knowledge about everything, though many of them only had about a tenth-grade education. They can tell me about the way things were when they were young, Chinese customs and things like that. But they also read the newspapers and keep up. I respect them very much. They work hard to put their children through college. And when that's over, I guess they'll retire because there won't be anyone to run the stores after them.

This excerpt suggests, as did other statements by the young, that the children of businessmen have little interest in taking over their father's grocery store. Young people think businessmen see them as loving, respectful, well-disciplined, obedient children who work diligently in school to bring their families honor, happiness, and joy.

Professionals

Professionals are their parents, brothers, sister, relatives, and friends who are viewed as successful, prosperous, independent, educated, and Americanized people. Professionals are also their role models. A young person defined professionals: "The professionals are a very successful group of people in the Delta. They are educated, independent, and looked upon highly in the Chinese community. We respect them and hope to be like them some day. We hope that maybe they will be able to do things for us, like help us find a job when we complete our education." Young people think professionals see them as secure, friendly, bright, studious, and well-disciplined youngsters who will eventually merge with them in the professional world.

College Students

College students are brothers, sisters, uncles, aunts, cousins, relatives, and friends who are struggling at school to become professionals. Young people see this group as lucky Americanized individuals who live away from home and are breaking away from the Chinese ways in a search for independence and acceptance in the wider world. One young person spoke about how college students gain independence:

> My older brother and sister are going to college now and they seem to be less and less tied down to the family. My father gives them more independence now than when they used to be at home. They kind of have a world of their own away from home because they have cars and can meet many new people. I guess that's where they pick up new ideas and become more like everyone else . . . and less like Chinese. Grandma says that.

We note also from this excerpt that old people pass on to the young people their own fears about the Americanization of college students with the purpose of delaying assimilation. Young people think college students see them as young, innocent, sheltered youngsters who must stay at home and wait their turn to go to college and thereby find out more about the world.

Women

Old women are grandmothers, mothers, aunts, relatives, and friends. Young people see them as respected, old-fashioned teachers and traditional Chinese homemakers. A young person spoke about old women's activities.

> The old women practice the Chinese customs in the Delta and try to teach them to young people. We always know when Chinese New Year is approaching because we have to pay up all of our debts, clean the house, and buy new clothes to wear on New Year's. The old women get together and talk a lot on the phone. They make tea pastries to eat. And they give us a red envelope of money to wish us luck in the new year. Its always kind of special that they make a big deal out of it. It brings everyone closer together.

Young people think that old women see them as respectful, obedient Chinese youngsters who are kind and considerate to them.

Young married women are mothers, sisters, aunts, relatives, and friends who are educated, loving, modern American homemakers. They claim that young married women made successful matches and are kind and attentive to their children. A young person remarked of this group: "They married good. Most married professionals and live in nice big homes. They treat their children with tender loving care and give them lots of attention. They are modern and keep up with the times. They seem to be very happy people. My sister is one, and she treats me real good." Young people think that young married women see them as the future leaders of their families and of the Chinese community and as honest, bright, intelligent, friendly, and well-behaved children.

Young unmarried women are sisters, aunts, relatives, and friends in the Chinese community. They are independent, educated, mobile, friendly Americanized individuals who are seeking professional careers and looking for mates. Girls of high school age identify strongly with this outspoken group. One young person commented:

> My sister finished college last summer and she's fixing to find someone to marry. She was never really interested in Chinese boys around here, so she's going to Memphis to find a job and look

for a boyfriend. Mother and father wouldn't let her date during college, so now she's looking. They tried to fix her up with a couple of Chinese boys, but it never worked. I think that if they would have left her alone, she would have found a boyfriend by now and got married. I hope she does find someone soon because she's got a pretty face but she's bottom heavy. All she did in college was study and eat. I know she will find a job but I don't know about a boyfriend. She is choosy.

Here we see again that the courtship situation of Chinese females is difficult. We also learn that the woman in this case is willing to make a break with her family and the Delta, a move that probably will increase her chances of marrying as well as her eventual assimilation. Young people think that young unmarried women see them as smart, sheltered, awkward, spoiled youngsters who do not understand the outside world. However, the youngsters know that they are loved by this group.

CHAPTER SEVEN

Conclusion: Dispersion

Much has been written about the efforts of various ethnic groups to retain a meaningful collective identity that encompasses a past, a present, and an uncertain future. People fashion, negotiate, and alter ethnic identities in relation to their aspirations, the views of other groups they must deal with, and the social and economic realities they face. The Mississippi Delta Chinese are no exception. Their community reference groups and identities are not based on idle dreams and wishes but rather have evolved from a history, from group experiences, expectations, and hard work—all related to the changing conditions they encounter.[1]

The first-generation Chinese pioneers discovered and developed an economic niche in biracial Delta society. The poor blacks needed neighborhood grocery stores because they lacked the capital to build their own, the credit to trade at white stores, and convenient economical transportation services to shopping areas. The Chinese grocery stores would never have opened or prospered in black neighborhoods without the cooperation and support of the black and white communities. This interdependence is often overlooked. The successful proprietors in time imported wives from China and established a church and mission school, which together with the ties fos-

---

[1]For an interesting parallel to the Chinese experience described here, see Kenji Ima, "Japanese Americans: The Making of Good People," in *Minority Report*, ed. Anthony G. Dworkin and Rosalind J. Dworkin (New York: Praeger 1976), pp. 254–295. Ima, who wrote about the Japanese Americans and their identities in relation to the wider society, found that Japanese Americans compelled themselves to develop new identities during the Americanization process. Other groups who have immigrated to the United States have behaved similarly. See Charles F. Marden and Gladys Meyer, *Minorities in American Society*, 5th ed. (New York: Van Nostrand, 1978).

tered by their businessess created a functional Delta Chinese community organized by the five reference groups, upon which the Delta Chinese fashioned their sense of collective identity. The economic foundation of this community, the independent Chinese grocer, is now disappearing for several interrelated reasons: (1) the original store owners are now growing old and retiring; (2) the new generation of Chinese has little interest in managing the family store; (3) stores are being sold rather than passing from father to son; (4) the status of blacks is changing; and (5) competition from large chain stores is eroding the business of small, family-owned stores. As property ceases to be handed down within the family, the economic basis for the traditional filial piety disappears as well.

Many of the third generation, far more educated and Americanized than members of the first two generations, do not find or expect to find the economic opportunities they are looking for in the Delta. Some of them wish to escape from a Mississippi Delta Chinese identity and from a community they see as outdated and restricting. Still others seek a "larger pool" of potential mates. These young adults do not have first-generation parents as a reference-group bridge upon which to build a strong Chinese identity. Second-generation parents are much more assimilated than the first, and parents of future generations will be even more Americanized. Increasing Americanization inevitably means greater geographic mobility; Americans are notorious for migrating in search of economic opportunities. Should the third generation move from the Delta, and should the inmigration of Chinese Americans or of Chinese immigrants remain a trickle, the community now existing will eventually disappear altogether.

Those who migrate from the Delta, for whatever reason and to whatever place, must build other kinds of identities, a process that will presumably entail recognition of other kinds of reference groups. In the latest generation of adults, males, particularly professionals, seem to adjust to the Chinese Delta community more easily than females, probably because: (1) males are more accepting of patriarchal society; (2) males are more traditional and less assimilated; (3) males have greater means and greater economic opportunities in the Delta; (4)

males are more in demand as mates and are therefore less likely to seek partners elsewhere. Even so, many Chinese men leave, and many more say they are going to leave. Males report two prime reasons for migrating and for planning to migrate: (1) to seek better positions, (2) to seek brides. Young male and female professionals and college students claim there is not a large enough group of young people in the Delta from which to select mates. Many say the parties they go to in the Delta are attended by small groups of people with whom they grew up, people they look upon as close friends rather than as potential spouses.

Young unmarried females in and out of college (members of the third generation) challenge the traditional views of the first two generations more than do other community members. This group appears particularly perceptive in assessing the identity problems of the Delta Chinese and is crucially significant to the future of the Delta Chinese community. Should appreciable numbers of this cohort leave and become assimilated into white society by intermarriage, the Delta Chinese community membership (already small) would be reduced drastically and would eventually cease to exist without outside replenishment. Outgroup intermarriage of any sort weakens any ethnic group. The outgroup marriage of males, however, is not as detrimental as that of females because ethnic males frequently bring their "outside brides" into the ethnic fold, whereas females often adopt their husband's ethnic identity. In the latter case the children of the female are lost forever. Female outmigrants, whether or not they intermarry, reduce the parent ethnic group more than do male outmigrants because females have the children.

Many Delta Chinese unmarried women seek independence from the Delta because they aspire to some other kind of identity in a white world. Some of these, probably most, would prefer to retain a symbolic Chinese reference point like that of some other Americans, who say, for example, "I am an American of French extraction." The problem with opting for this strategy is the racial aspect of "extraction." In the United States, Europeans are defined as white, whereas immigrants from the Far East are not, as census documents show, nor are their children, despite U.S. citizenship. To unmarried (and to some married) college and professional women, migration from the Delta offers more opportunity for independence and for economic and social equality in a wider, freer, and more challenging world. Many prefer not to marry Delta Chinese males because they wish to avoid, in their words, "the same old thing." Some seek assimilation and integration into white society by attending white coeducational colleges and universities, joining white Protestant churches, affiliating with white clubs (when they can), entering white professional organizations, working with whites in the public sector, making friendships with whites, moving to white neighborhoods, dating whites, and in some cases marrying whites—simultaneously disassociating themselves from strictly Delta Chinese social organizations and affairs. Many have already moved from the Delta, where they intentionally cultivate professional and social relationships with whites. Still, some others marry Delta Chinese males who seem to be assimilated as they themselves are.

The women of the third generation know that the triethnic community in which the old people established themselves has worked to their advantage in the past because it has obviated classification as "colored." Currently, some claim that the Delta community is repressive to further upward mobility and that it offers limited job opportunities. Others note racial problems (past and present) that stem from power plays by whites and blacks which have "sandwiched the Chinese in the middle." They affirm that the whites do not support them in their efforts to maintain a Chinese identity and that this lack of affirmation might lead to the loss of ethnic status and Chinese identity. This eventuality, of course, appears highly unlikely.

Some single professional and college women see themselves as marginal people, "not colored, not quite white, but still not black." One college coed perceptively described the view some members of this group held of the rigidity and unfairness of the triethnic society and the associated identity problems.

> Maybe in the beginning it was necessary to assert our Chineseness to get away from being classified and treated as colored people. But now the time has come to reclassify our standing. We are white-educated, born and bred Mississippi taxpayers caught in

the middle of supporting both ends of the racial stick. But everything is still based on being black or white, and this is the latter
part of the twentieth century! Some of my white friends call me
the Delta lotus. I'm a Delta Southerner, but still a lotus and not
a magnolia. I guess I can never be one because when I look in the
mirror I don't have lily-white skin. But it sure ain't black, either.
It's a God-awful in-between shade of destiny. Just cause I'm not
white in the Delta doesn't mean I can't be white somewhere else
. . ., or maybe I can even be Chinese in another place, but not in
the Delta.

This is probably the most significant statement I have quoted
because it succinctly expresses the marginality that many third-
generation women, the mothers of future generations, feel is
associated with their position. Some of these women, then, do
not have a strong Delta Chinese identity and feel blocked in an
attempt to acquire a white one. Whites in the Delta partially
accept them but avoid intimate ties. The Delta Chinese attempt to suppress any identification with blacks or black culture
in a quest for white upward social mobility (for example, body
language, humor, speech patterns, emotional expression,
and argot acquired from blacks in the family business milieu
and at school). Whites likewise deny the influence of black
culture.[2]

A number of young Chinese women envision conflict with
the old people, wives of businessmen, and parents concerning
such issues as ethnic solidarity, femininity, religion, filial piety,
living arrangements, job sites, dress, public demeanor, dating,
mate selection, courtship practices, marriage, and mobility.
They are beginning to demand equal treatment with their
brothers in the Delta Chinese family and appear to be slowly
achieving success in the areas of personal worth and family

[2]It appears to the authors that whites, blacks, and Delta Chinese share experiences of Southern culture much more similar than they realize or admit.
Whites, Chinese, and blacks tell and laugh at the same joke forms whose meta-
phorical symbolism involves religious, sexual, animal, and racial themes (the
ethnic subjects switch, depending on the ethnic identity of the speaker). The
three groups show many similarities in speech patterns, religion, body movement, music appreciation, diet, recreational pursuits, patriotic feelings, regional
sense of place, and consciousness of time, family, and continuity. And all, of
course, are Southerners.

decision making.[3] Despite this progress, many leave the Delta before consolidating their gains. These women make it clear to other community group members (by attitudes and behavior) that they will no longer accept the subordinate status granted them by the Chinese patriarchy. One college coed asserted her views about sexuality, independence, dating, marriage, and the need to leave the Delta in order to achieve sexual, economic, and social equality:

> To me virginity is no big thing these days, but Chinese parents keep emphasizing the "good girl" image. And as far as dating is concerned, I date whomever I please. I don't pay any attention to the gossip network because what I do is my own business. The same goes for courtship and marriage. I'll choose who I want to marry, not some jerk my parents think up in Hong Kong or something. I will leave the Delta when I graduate to find a well-paying job. I want to live my own life, make my own decisions, and find myself . . ., get some objectivity. And to do that I have to leave the Delta. I don't want to wind up married to so-and-so, pregnant, and a slave to the Chinese ways. There is no profit sticking around here for me.

This excerpt indicates a very strong position, one that is not taken by all unmarried young women. Still, it does seem to reflect to some extent the attitudes, if not the behavior, of many.

Chinese-white marriages are frowned upon by the oldest Delta Chinese and the Delta whites.[4] Nevertheless, some Chinese reluctantly accept the marriage of their daughters to white professionals. A few Chinese males are married to white females in the Delta, and in these few cases the females become Chinese in the eyes of whites. I received no reports on Chinese females married to working-class whites or to blacks. Intermar-

[3]Rarely do Delta Chinese women—or for that matter, Southern women and men—subscribe to the women's movement, although this movement probably focuses more on helping people find self-awareness than on breaking down traditional sex role stereotypes and categories.

[4]Many community members reported that many mixed marriages ended in divorce. This is probably true. Mixed marriages generally are more likely to end in divorce than ingroup marriages, although prevailing national trends suggest that more is involved than the individuals' ethnic identities.

riage usually means that Chinese females marry white males. Mixed married couples live outside the Delta in most cases.

One Delta Chinese school teacher recalled her marital decision, parental and community reaction, and a quest for sexual equality by leaving the Delta:

> It wasn't an easy decision to make marrying outside the Chinese community, but that was the way I felt. I wanted to marry John because I got along better with him than I did with the Chinese boys. They didn't interest me at all. At first my family didn't accept our marriage. Rumors floated around the Delta that I had married "one of them." But I didn't listen to that. I wasn't around. We lived in Florida then. After a while my family realized that the marriage was working out and that I was happy, so they weren't opposed to it anymore. I think John's social standing had a lot to do with my family accepting our marriage. Because he's a college professor. He is educated and my parents like that. They wouldn't have gone for a redneck marriage. So the only way a Chinese woman is going to exercise full sexual freedom . . . and a chance to find a good job and meet interesting people is to leave the Delta. My children will be white, not Chinese.

Professional and college women appear to be on the way to achieving altered identities in the white world by way of education, careers, mobility (movement from the Delta), some intermarriage with whites, and marriage to Americanized Delta Chinese. Those who remain in the Delta are gaining some independence but still endure identity problems and intergenerational strife. Old people, businessmen and their wives, some young married people, and young children support the triethnic society, though not to the same degree. Though most young people voice support for this system, they also express desires to leave after they graduate from college.

Though parents express ambivalence about their children's need to leave, they resign themselves to the inevitable. As one Chinese mother explained: "You can't keep them at home for very long, not even for a few days during vacation. They got to leave because their professions demand it. If there were better opportunities here they might stay, but there ain't, we older people know that. And they want more freedom now. The Delta's too small for them."

Should the third generation continue to leave the Delta (which is likely) and the immigration of Chinese remain insignificant (which is likely), the Chinese Delta community membership will disperse. Significantly, however, reports from members of all Delta Chinese community groups attest to the fact that the young who leave do not go far. Many males and females move to Jackson, Memphis, and Houston, where some are said to maintain their Mississippi Chinese identity. Conceivably, these migrants could establish Chinese-American communities in these cities in some respects similar to that of the Delta homeland. This eventuality will depend on the young immigrants themselves. It is highly unlikely that many Delta Chinese will migrate to large, distant Chinese enclaves such as San Francisco, Los Angeles, Chicago, and New York because they are quite different in cultural traits from the Chinese Americans in these settlements. They are Southerners. I received few reports about Delta migrants to these areas, and these few indicated that the Delta Chinese migrants were not well received. Of course, there are some exceptions.

Though my research indicates that assimilation and dispersion of the Delta Chinese is occuring rapidly, the Chinese themselves will determine the extent to which the pattern holds true. Whatever happens, a Protestant religious orientation, strong family ties, frugality and the work ethic, parental respect, law-abiding behavior, emotional control, careful living habits (little smoking, drinking, drugs), an emphasis on education, Chinese aesthetic appreciation, and a symbolic Chinese identity—all of which are elements of the Delta culture—will probably persist. The Chinese in the Delta as in many other parts of the world have established a rich cultural legacy, and all Mississippians are the beneficiaries of this gift.

My findings also suggest that the fate of other ethnic enclaves (of whatever origin) will be similar if they face the following adverse conditions: (1) transplantation in small numbers over time into a foreign, isolated milieu far away from the mother country and large well-established ethnic centers (so that they lack the benefit of cultural reinforcement); (2) the exchange of an ethnic religious orientation and language for a host religion and language; (3) steady outmigration; (4) a lack of steady ethnic inmigration; (5) disruptions of the primary economic base; (6) strong identification with the dominant group in the host country and surrender to an assimilation process including intermarriage; (7) loss of an older ethnic generation without assumption of its role by a new generation. Such isolated ethnic communities will also probably produce some people in search of new identities who are conscious of feeling marginal. Individuals torn between two or more cultures, though somewhat alienated, are often more perceptive about a society than are those conscious of belonging, because they stand on the outside and look in.[5] Such misfits can also stand partially inside and look out. All societies require such people; in many cases they are able to take a more objective stance toward events and issues than can insiders fully committed to the status quo. Finally, people who feel marginal do not necessarily remain so. Many eventually discover strong, supporting identities. The Mississippi Delta Chinese will find their own identities in their own way. But those Chinese who remain in the Delta will probably always be lotus among the magnolias.

[5]See Alfred Schutz's illuminating essays: Alfred Schutz, "The Stranger: An Essay in Social Psychology," *American Journal of Sociology,* vol. 49, no. 6 (1944), pp. 499–507; and "The Homecomer," *American Journal of Sociology,* vol. 50, no. 5 (1945), pp. 369–376.

Selected Bibliography

Ball, Donald W. "An Abortion Clinic Ethnography." *Social Problems* (1967), pp. 293–301.

————. *Microecology: Social Situations and Intimate Space.* New York: Bobbs-Merrill, 1973.

Barth, Gunther. *Bitter Strength: A History of the Chinese in the United States, 1850–1870.* Cambridge, Mass.: Harvard University Press, 1964.

Becker, Howard S. "Problems of Inference and Proof in Participant Observation." *American Sociological Review* 23 (December 1958), pp. 652–660.

————. "The Relevance of Life Histories." In *Sociological Methods: A Sourcebook,* ed. Norman K. Denzin, pp. 419–428. Chicago: Aldine, 1970.

Becker, Howard S., and Blanche Geer. "Participant Observation and Interviewing: A Comparison." *Human Organization* (1957), pp. 28–32.

Bellman, Beryl L., and Bennetta Jules-Rosette. *A Paradigm for Looking: Cross-Cultural Research with Visual Media.* Norwood, N. J.: Ablex, 1977.

Berger, Peter L., and Thomas Luckmann. *The Social Construction of Reality.* Garden City: Doubleday, 1966.

Berreman, Gerald D. "Caste in India and the United States." *American Journal of Sociology,* vol. 66, no. 1 (July 1960), pp. 120–127.

Berry, Brewton. *Almost White.* London: Collier-Macmillan, 1963.

Blauner, Robert. "Colonized and Immigrant Minorities." In *Racial Oppression in America.* New York: Harper and Row, 1972.

————. Book review of Loewen's *The Mississippi Chinese, American Journal of Sociology,* vol. 79, no. 2 (September 1973), pp. 486–487.

Blumer, Herbert. *Symbolic Interactionism: Perspective and Method.* Englewood Cliffs, N.J.: Prentice-Hall, 1969.

Bonacich, Edna. "A Theory of Middleman Minorities." *American Sociological Review* 38 (October 1973), pp. 583–594.

Brandfon, Robert L. *Cotton Kingdom of the New South.* Cambridge, Mass.: Harvard University Press, 1967.

Bruyn, Severyn T. *The Human Perspective in Sociology: The Methodology of Participant Observation.* Englewood Cliffs, N.J.: Prentice-Hall, 1966.

————. "The Methodology of Participant Observation." In *Qualitative Methodology: Firsthand Involvement with the Social World,* ed. William J. Filstead, pp. 305–327. Chicago: Markham, 1970.

Buchler, Justus. *The Concept of Method.* New York: Columbia University Press, 1961.

Byers, Paul. "Still Photography in the Systematic Recording and Analysis of Behavioral Data." *Human Organization* 22 (1963), pp. 78–84.

Cash, W. J. *The Mind of the South.* New York: Alfred A. Knopf, 1941.

Chan, Kit-Mui Leung. "Assimilation of the Chinese Americans in the Mississippi Delta." Master's Thesis, Mississippi State University, Starkville, 1969.

Chow, Gay. "Yellow in a Black and White World: A Delta Chinese Looks at a History of the Delta Chinese." Book review of Loewen's *The Mississippi Chinese. The Reflector,* vol. 85, no. 28 (January 16, 1973), p. 3.

Clinard, Marshall B., and Richard Quinney. *Criminal Behavior Systems: A Typology.* 2nd ed. New York: Holt, Rinehart and Winston, 1973.

Collier, John, Jr. *Visual Anthropology: Photography as a Research Method.* New York: Holt, Rinehart and Winston, 1967.

Coolidge, Mary. *Chinese Immigration.* New York: Henry Holt, 1909.

Cowie, James B., and Julian B. Roebuck. *An Ethnography of a Chiropractice Clinic: Definitions of a Deviant Situation.* New York: Free Press, 1975.

Davis, Allison, B. B. Gardner, and M. R. Gardner. *Deep South.* Chicago: University of Chicago Press, 1941.

Denzin, Norman K. *The Research Act.* Chicago: Aldine, 1970.

Dewey, John. *Human Nature and Social Conduct.* New York: Bedminster Press, 1922.

Dollard, John. *Caste and Class in a Southern Town.* New Haven: Yale University Press, 1937.

Douglas, Jack, ed. *Understanding Everyday Life: Toward the Reconstruction of Sociological Knowledge.* Chicago: Aldine, 1967.

Dumont, Louis. *Homo Hierarchicus: The Caste System and Its Implications.* Trans. Mark Sainsbury. Chicago: University of Chicago Press, 1970.

Edgerton, Robert B., and L. L. Langness. *Methods and Styles in the Study of Culture.* San Francisco: Chandler and Sharp, 1974.

Erikson, Erik. "The Concept of Identity in Race Relations: Notes and Queries." *Daedalus* 95 (winter 1966), pp. 145–171.

Fong, Stanley L. M. "Assimilation of Chinese in America: Changes in Orientation and Social Perception." *American Journal of Sociology* 81 (1965), pp. 265–273.

Garfinkel, Harold. *Studies in Ethnomethodology*. Englewood Cliffs, N.J.: Prentice-Hall, 1967.

Goffman, Erving. *The Presentation of Self in Everyday Life*. Garden City: Doubleday, 1959.

Goldstein, Kenneth S. *A Guide For Field Workers in Folklore*. Hatboro, Pa.: Folklore Associates, 1964.

Gordon, Milton M. "Assimilation in America: Theory and Reality." *Daedalus* 90 (Spring 1961), pp. 263–285.

Handlin, Oscar. *The Uprooted*. New York: Grosset and Dunlap, 1951.

Hertzler, Joyce O. *A Sociology of Language*. New York: Random House, 1965.

Hewitt, John P. *Self and Society: A Symbolic Interactionist Social Psychology*. Boston: Allyn and Bacon, 1976.

Hsu, Francis L. K. *Americans and Chinese: Two Ways of Life*. New York: Schuman, 1953.

——. *The Challenge of the American Dream: The Chinese in the United States*. Belmont, Calif.: Wadsworth, 1971.

Husserl, Edmund. *Ideas: General Introduction to Pure Phenomenology*. Trans. W. R. Boyce Gibson. London: G. Allen and Unwin, 1913.

——. *The Phenomenology of Internal Time-Consciousness*. Ed. Martin Heidegger. Trans. James S. Churchill. Bloomington: Indiana University Press, 1964.

Irwin, John. *The Felon*. Englewood Cliffs, N.J.: Prentice-Hall, 1970.

Killian, Lewis M. "Herbert Blumer's Contribution to Race Relations." In *Human Nature and Collective Behavior*. New Brunswick, N.J.: Transaction Books, 1970.

——. *White Southerners*. New York: Random House, 1970.

Kim, Choong Soon. *An Asian Anthropologist in the South*. Knoxville: University of Tennessee Press, 1977.

King, Florence. "The Good Ole Boy." *Harper's Magazine* 248 (April 1974), pp. 78–82.

Kingston, Maxine Hong. *The Woman Warrior*. New York: Vintage Books, 1975.

——. *China Men*. New York: Alfred A. Knopf, 1976.

Kuo, Chia-Ling. "The Chinese on Long Island—A Pilot Study." *Phylon* (1970), pp. 282–287.

Ladner, Heber. *Mississippi Official Statistical Register, 1972–1976*. Jackson, Miss.: Office of the Secretary of State, 1976.

Lee, Rose Hum. *The Chinese in the United States of America*. Hong Kong: Hong Kong University Press, 1960.

Lee, Virginia Winkleman. "For the Delta—Nation's First Chinese Community Education Center." *Memphis Commercial Appeal*, February 14, 1937.

LeMasters, E. E. *Blue-Collar Aristocrats: Life-Styles at a Working-Class Tavern*. Wisconsin: University of Wisconsin Press, 1975.

Loewen, James W. *The Mississippi Chinese: Between Black and White.* Cambridge, Mass.: Harvard University Press, 1971.

Lyman, Stanford Morris. "Spectrum of Color." *Social Research,* vol. 31, no. 3 (1964), pp. 364–373.

————. "The Race Relations Cycle of Robert E. Park." *Pacific Sociological Review* 11 (spring 1968), pp. 16–22.

————. *Chinese Americans.* New York: Random House, 1974.

Lyman, Stanford Morris, and Marvin B. Scott. *A Sociology of the Absurd.* New York: Appleton-Century-Crofts, 1980.

Malinowski, Bronislaw. *Argonauts of the Western Pacific.* London: Routledge, 1922.

McCall, George J., and J. L. Simmons. *Identities and Interactions.* New York: Free Press, 1966.

Mead, George Herbert. *The Philosophy of the Act.* Chicago: University of Chicago Press, 1938.

————. *The Philosophy of the Present.* Chicago: Open Court, 1938.

Mencken, H. L. *A Mencken Chrestomathy.* New York: Alfred A. Knopf, 1967.

Messinger, Sheldon L., Harold Sampson, and Robert D. Towne. "Life as Theater: Some Notes on the Dramaturgic Approach." *Sociometry* (1962), pp. 98–110.

Mills, C. Wright. *The Sociological Imagination.* New York: Oxford University Press, 1959.

Moore, Barrington, Jr. *The Social Origins of Dictatorship and Democracy: Lord and Peasant in the Making of the Modern World.* Boston: Beacon Press, 1966.

Nee, Victor G., and Brett De Bary Nee. *Longtime Californ': A Documentary Study of an American Chinatown.* New York: Pantheon Books, 1972.

O'Brien, Robert W. "Status of the Chinese in the Mississippi Delta." *Social Forces* (March 1941), pp. 386–390.

Park, Robert Ezra. *Race and Culture.* Glencoe: Free Press, 1950.

Peterson, John H., Jr. "Assimilation, Separation, and Outmigration in an American Indian Group." *American Anthropologist* 74 (1972), pp. 1286–1295.

Quan, Robert Seto. "The Creation, Maintenance, and Dissolution of Mississippi Delta Chinese Identities." *Bulletin, Chinese Historical Society of America,* vol. 16, nos. 3,4,5,6 (March-June 1981).

Roebuck, Julian B., and Wolfgang Frese. *The Rendezvous: A Case Study of an After-Hours Club.* New York: Free Press, 1976.

Rummel, George A. III. "The Delta Chinese: An Exploratory Study in Assimilation." Master's Thesis, University of Mississippi, Oxford, 1966.

Rummel, George A. III, and Betty Price. "A Vanishing Culture." *Mississippi Magazine* (1965), pp. 14–16.

Saltz, David. "Public Apology Still Demanded." *Delta Democrat-Times,* August 6, 1978, p. 1.

Sapir, Edward. "The Status of Linguistics as a Science." *Language* 5 (1929), pp. 209–210.

Schutz, Alfred. "The Stranger: An Essay in Social Psychology." *American Journal of Sociology,* vol. 49, no. 6 (1944), pp. 499–507.

———. "The Homecomer." *American Journal of Sociology,* vol. 50, no. 5 (1945), pp. 369–376.

Shibutani, Tamotsu. "Reference Groups as Perspectives." *American Journal of Sociology* 60 (May 1955), pp. 562–570.

Shibutani, Tamotsu, and Kian M. Kwan. *Ethnic Stratification: A Comparative Approach.* New York: Macmillan, 1965.

Silver, James W. *Mississippi: The Closed Society.* New York: Harcourt, Brace and World, 1963.

Simmel, Georg. *The Sociology of Georg Simmel.* Trans. Kurt H. Wolff. New York: Free Press, 1950.

Siu, Paul C. P. "The Sojourner." *American Journal of Sociology* 58 (July 1952), pp. 33–44.

Smith, Frank E. *The Yazoo River.* Rinehart, 1954.

Steel, C. Hoy. "The Acculturation Model in Indian Studies: A Critique." In *Majority and Minority: The Dynamics of Racial and Ethinic Relations,* ed. Norman R. Yetman and C. Hoy Steel, pp. 305–314. Boston: Allyn and Bacon, 1975.

Sung, Betty Lee. *Mountain of Gold: The Story of the Chinese in America.* New York: Macmillan, 1967.

U.S. Department of Commerce, Bureau of the Census. *1970 Census of Population,* PC (S1)-11. Washington, D.C.: U.S. Government Printing Office, 1972.

United States Reports. *Cases Adjudged in the Supreme Court at October Term* (1927). *Gong Lum et al.* v. *Rice et al.,* 275:78–82. See also Mississippi Reports (1925). *Rice* v. *Gong Lum,* appeal to the Mississippi Supreme Court, 139:760–763.

Veblen, Thorstein B. *The Theory of the Leisure Class: An Economic Study of Institutions.* New York: Modern Library, 1899.

Vidich, Arthur J., and Gilbert Shapiro. "A Comparison of Participant Observation and Survey Data." *American Sociological Review* 20 (February 1955), pp. 28–33.

Von Hoffman, Nicholas. *Mississippi Notebook.* New York: David White, 1964.

Webb, Eugene. *Unobtrusive Measures: Nonreactive Research in the Social Sciences.* Chicago: Rand McNally, 1966.

Welty, Eudora. *One Time: One Place.* New York: Randon House, 1971.

Wong, Bernard. "Social Stratification, Adaptive Strategies, and the Chinese Community of New York." *Urban Life: A Journal of Ethnographic Research,* vol. 5, no. 1 (April 1976), pp. 33–52.

Wong, Charles Choy. "Ethnicity, Work, and Community: The Case of Chinese in Los Angeles." Ph.D. Dissertation, University of California, Los Angeles, 1979.

Worth, Sol, and John Adair. *Through Navaho Eyes.* Bloomington: Indiana University Press, 1972.

Zakia, Richard D. *Perception and Photography.* Englewood Cliffs, N.J.: Prentice-Hall, 1975.

Zelditch, Morris, Jr. "Some Methodological Problems of Field Studies." *American Journal of Sociology* 67 (March 1962), pp. 566–576.

Index

161